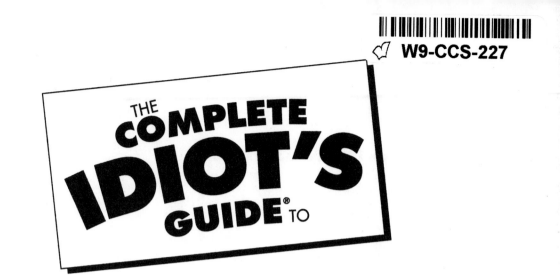

THE **COMPLETE IDIOT'S GUIDE®** TO

Sensual Massage

by Dr. Patti Britton and Helen Hodgson

ALPHA

A member of Penguin Group (USA) Inc.

We dedicate this book to all people who hunger for human touch and to the 40 million Americans who suffer in no-sex or low-sex marriages. May this book enliven your pleasure and bring you healing.

Publisher: *Marie Butler-Knight*
Product Manager: *Phil Kitchel*
Senior Managing Editor: *Jennifer Chisholm*
Acquisitions Editor: *Gary Goldstein*
Development Editor: *Jennifer Moore*
Production Editor: *Billy Fields*
Copy Editor: *Cari Luna*
Illustrator: *Chris Eliopoulos*
Photographer: *Robert Dunlap, assisted by Claes Lilja*
Cover/Book Designer: *Trina Wurst*
Indexer: *Aamir Burki*
Layout/Proofreading: *Angela Calvert, Mary Hunt*

Contents at a Glance

Appendixes

Contents

Foreword

From the moment we nuzzle into our mother's breast, to the hour of our death, nothing offers more comfort or tenderness than human touch. Touch is the unspoken way we can communicate with everyone we love. But perhaps the people we touch most, or at least would like to touch most, are our intimate partners. Not only does skin-to-skin contact create a deeper sense of connection, it can stimulate pleasure, inspire the tingle of romance, and unleash the electricity of eroticism.

Touching is good for our health, hearts, and souls, as well as our love lives. This book shows us how to be "better touchers," as it guides us through the wonderful ways we can bring sensual massage into our daily life.

Massage reduces stress, promotes relaxation, and sets the stage for releasing our troubles—it liberates us to feel freer in our own skin. Sensual massage adds intimacy and pleasure to this experience, providing us with a forum to express our feelings and receive nurturing and loving touch. It is a way to connect deeply with another person on many levels.

In these pages you will find an insightful and comprehensive guide filled with easy-to-follow tips and lots of encouragement for making massage natural and fun. It will take you from the history of massage to the wide spectrum of pleasures and possibilities that sensual massage offers today. It outlines *everything you need to know* to bring sensual massage into your life and relationships. You'll learn to approach sensual massage from many perspectives, depending on your needs and desires at the moment: for play or healing, emotional soothing or sexual sizzle, pure spirituality or mind blowing orgasms.

There are no better experts to bring all of this information to you in an easy to understand guide than Dr. Patti Britton and Helen Hodgson. Dr. Patti, a sexologist and sex coach, has long been empowering men and women to discover the healing and rejuvenating power of pleasure. She brings heart, soul, and spirituality to this very sexy topic—and she knows her stuff! "Goddess" Helen Hodgson is professional massage therapist who describes many massage techniques that you can safely perform at home in addition to offering insights into the physiological and emotional nuances of touch. Together, Dr. Patti and Goddess Helen have outlined an extensive array sensual delights.

Make up your mind that it is time to bring more pleasure into your life: Set aside some time for you and your beloved. Play some soft music, light a candle, add your favorite flowers and scents … and whip out the massage oil.

The Complete Idiot's Guide to Sensual Massage offers a step-by-step approach to putting the pep back into relationships or bringing new lovers closer. Whether you enter into your sacred time of shared pleasure like a God and Goddess celebrating the holy temple of their bodies, or just approach it like playmates ready for a night of pleasure, it will change your life!

—Laurie Sue Brockway

Author of *A Goddess Is a Girl's Best Friend: A Divine Guide to Finding Love, Success, and Happiness* (Perigee Books, December 2002)

Introduction

If you are looking for the perfect solution to feeling disconnected from your partner, are stressed or tired all the time, long for skin-to-skin touch, wish sex would happen more often, or just wanna have more fun in your life, this book's for you. This is the ultimate massage guidebook, with many exercises to propel you along the pathway to pleasure through sensual touch.

In this book, we will show you how to prepare your surroundings, your body, your mind, *and* your spirit for your massage experience. Of course, you'll also find out how to do some basic and not-so-basic strokes and how to position yourself to avoid strain and maximize energy. And while we encourage you to use verbal and nonverbal communication (what we call body talk) as a roadmap for you sensual journey, we also provide you with step-by-step instructions for a full-body massage.

Most humans are starved for touch of any kind. So when people actually take the time to learn how to connect with each other body-to-body, magic happens. That magic can range from increased health and physical well-being, pure pleasure from touch itself, and even a better sex life. (We did say in our letter on the inside front cover that this is the ultimate foreplay to foreplay book didn't we? You just might find that sensual massage is the healthy injection that your relationship has been needing!)

Please take the journey with us, one stroke at a time, and remember to be patient with yourself and your lucky massage mate. It takes time and dedication to learn how to be a good sensual touch giver and receiver, but this is one task where practice feels oh-so-good.

How This Book Is Organized

Part 1, "The Beauty of Massage," will take you through the history of massage, explain various massage techniques such as shiatsu and Swedish massage, and provide you with a list of everything you'll need to get started. You'll find out all about massage oils, how to prepare your body for massage, what tools you'll want on hand, and some basic massage do's and don'ts.

Part 2, "Let's Touch!" shows you how to do the delicious deed. Body up and body down, you are going to explore all of the different and unique ways to make the body feel refreshed, relaxed, and just plain *good*. In addition, of course, you'll get to practice the four basic strokes and play around with body positioning and alignment. Finally, you're going to find out how to use massage to help you through challenging life experiences, like pregnancy, illness, and growing older.

Part 3, "Sensual Stagings," is all about preparation. Here you'll find out how to pick the best massage location for your needs and how to light and decorate your surroundings to create the appropriate mood. You'll also find out how to use music, aromas, food, and visual cues to stimulate all of the senses.

Part 4, "Beyond Touch," explores the emotional benefits of touch and how to overcome obstacles to intimacy. In addition, you'll explore the spiritual side of massage and learn the importance of discussing with your partner what you each want out of the massage.

Part 5, "Going Wild," takes massage to a new level. Here you'll find out the many ways that massage can be used as an arousal technique. The final chapter helps you maximize your massage experience even *after* it's over.

Sensual Sidebars

You'll find the following sidebars throughout this book:

Finger Tip

Maximize your massage experience by following these tips.

Ouch!

Warnings and watchouts for your safety.

Dr. Patti Says
Here you'll find insights on sexuality, relationships, and personal well-being from a sex doc's point of view.

Goddess Helen Says
Words of advice from a true expert on touch.

Touch Term

So that you don't have to stop in the middle of your massage to run and look up a word, we've provided definitions to technical and some not-so-technical terms.

Acknowledgments

A book like this would never exist if it weren't for the precious gifts of our clients, who let us delve so deeply into their personal lives. They are the true inspiration for our work. We want to say a special thank you to Luis Lerma T., whose caricatures and ideas helped inspire our words, and the talented photographer/filmmaker Robert Dunlap, whose images made our ideas sizzle! We extend our appreciation to our amazing models—Rachel Capata, Gene and Trista Segal, Kevin Dailey, Martha Ellen Senseney, and Bruce and Jocelyn McCormick—along with our skillful illustrator, Hrana Janto. Thanks to our wondrous warrior literary agent, Jessica Faust, who saved the day, and to all of the players at Alpha Books who helped to make this project manifest our deepest dreams for your pleasure.

Trademarks

All terms mentioned in this book that are known to be or are suspected of being trademarks or service marks have been appropriately capitalized. Alpha Books and Penguin Group (USA) Inc. cannot attest to the accuracy of this information. Use of a term in this book should not be regarded as affecting the validity of any trademark or service mark.

Part 1

The Beauty of Massage

People have been massaging each other for pleasure and health since the dawn of human history. Let's take a look at the touch techniques they've developed over time, from ancient Eastern practices such as shiatsu and acupressure to more modern systems such as Swedish massage. We'll then explore the continuum of touch and find out where sensual massage—touch for the sake of pleasure—fits in.

Chapter 1

Back Over Time

In This Chapter

- ◆ The origins of massage for healing purposes
- ◆ Touch techniques around the world
- ◆ Cool facts in the history of massage
- ◆ Where massage is today

Human touch is as old as life itself.

Imagine yourself back in the good old days of the cave dwellers. There's Grud, on his way home from slaying a wooly mammoth, hauling the monstrous creature's carcass. There's Ila, mother to his children, sitting in the glacial cave, just returned from gathering brush and berries from the surrounding wilderness. As darkness begins to fall, Ila turns to Grud and whispers, "Maybe later we do the touch thing?" He grunts back a friendly "Ugh," then turns his attention to carving meat off the mammoth.

Ooga Booga! One Touch Is Worth a Thousand Words

After all their offspring are tucked under their furs, with the fire casting a warm glow on them, Grud and Ila lie together and tenderly touch each other's bodies. Grud bites into a wild apple to sweeten his breath, then draws Ila's mouth to him, sharing the sweet morsel of fruit and heightening her olfactory senses. Next, she applies the oil of musk ox to his flesh, softening his rough skin. He lies quietly under the wrap with her, allowing her fingers to penetrate his tired muscles, yet understanding this to be her signal for romance.

The primal oohs and ahs from cave men and women enjoying their sensual massages were probably some of the first sounds of pleasure uttered in those early human settlements.

Curses, Bones, and Trinkets: Ancient Cultures of Massage

As humans evolved, so did their touch techniques. For example, archaeologists have found stone probes in Chinese caves and tombs that were used to soothe aches and pains. Loved ones, it seems, would lay the tools against sore muscles and the soles of the feet, thereby relieving aches and pains throughout the body. Humans were beginning to discover the inner universe of the body, including the sources of their discomforts and even diseases.

Mongolian horsemen were also known to use stones to relax tense muscles. Before going into battle, the warriors would receive a stone massage, during which their fears, believed to be trapped inside their muscles, would be released. When all the muscles were loose and relaxed, the warriors were ready for battle. So even in ancient times, massage was much more than a physical relaxant—it helped to heal the body and embolden the spirit.

Finger Tip

The primitive stone massage probes found in Chinese caves are forebears of acupuncture needles. Those stone massages were early forms of the acupressure massage.

Soon other early massage techniques began to sprout up around the globe.

Don't Asp Me! Egypt and Cleopatra

Egyptian hieroglyphs, which date from 2500 B.C.E., are filled with depictions of Egyptians receiving an early form of *reflexology*. Somehow the Egyptians had discovered that tension in any part of the feet reflected stress clusters in corresponding parts of the body. These corresponding parts have appeared in drawings and charts as far back as the building of the Egyptian pyramids. The simple act of giving a foot rub began to take on deeper meaning.

Touch Term

Vladamir Bekterev first referred to the science of reflex therapy as "reflexology" in 1917. **Reflexology** is a therapy in which the feet or hands are pressed to bring relief to corresponding areas of the body.

No doubt the Egyptian queen Cleopatra knew of massage and used it along with her ravishing beauty to seduce Julius Caesar. It is said that Cleopatra went to great lengths to understand all the sensual desires of a man. She spent her days plying men with wine and women until she seduced her prey, always exceeding his sensual expectations.

And Cleopatra knew that all the senses could be used to invoke sensuality. When the black beauty sailed down the Nile to seduce Caesar's rival, Marc Anthony, she soaked the sails of her ship in the scent of jasmine to perfume the night air, leaving a trail of seduced admirers. Her barge was lined with the most beautiful of her women, exquisitely attired maidens who also pulled the oars and controlled the sails. On the deck of the barge a massive incense burner was kept aflame with heaps of Kyphi, the richest of Egyptian scented offerings. They mixed oils of cassia, cinnamon, peppermint, pistacia, juniper, acacia, henna, and cypress, then soaked the aromatic mixture in wine and added honey, resins, and myrrh. Can't you just picture the barge floating as if on a cloud of sensual intoxication, mesmerizing all the men she passed by?

Goddess Helen Says

Cleopatra was known for her beauty, including her beautiful skin. Try one of Cleopatra's milk baths—it is a great remedy for dry, itchy, and nutrient-deficient skin. First take a shower, then prepare a warm bath with 2 cups of whole milk, 2 cups of powdered milk, and 5 to 10 drops of your favorite scented oils. Then lay and soak, relaxing for about 20 minutes. Next, gently dry yourself and apply a moisturizer with vitamin E or natural aloe vera.

While Cleopatra was relaxing in her bath, musicians played ambient music. Afterward she would have a maiden remove any excess hair, apply henna for eyeliner and specially prepared makeup that enhanced the beauty of her skin and at the same time protected it from the harmful rays of the sun.

Once on board her vessel, so the tale goes, Marc Anthony fell prey to Cleopatra's charms. While "holding court" with the lovely queen (we're being polite here), Marc

Anthony reportedly reached out and began to massage Cleopatra's manicured toes and oiled feet. We don't believe for a second that he stopped there, but you can fill in the blanks. Poor Marc Anthony never stood a chance.

Those Decadent Romans!

Asclepiades, a Greek physician, brought massage to Rome. It wasn't long before it was part of the Roman lifestyle. Servants massaged the rich in their homes, while the average Roman went to the public baths for his touch treatment. Massage became the essential treatment for all that ailed the receiver. Those imaginative Romans even believed that massage could replace exercise and the harmful effects from overindulgence in alcohol. If only that were true!

Finger Tip

Julius Caesar suffered from many nervous disorders including epilepsy. According to legend, if not for his daily massages—or "pinching" as they called it—Caesar would not have been able to carry on as leader of Rome.

Goddess Helen Says

The Romans made massage popular, but it was the Greek men of medicine—such as Homer, Asclepiades, and Hippocrates— who introduced it to them.

Romans used full-body massage to arouse the senses and nerves, to make the joints limber, and to improve circulation. They rubbed very fine oil all over their bodies to keep the skin supple and young-looking, as well as fragrant.

Galen, a physician to several emperors of the first century C.E., including Julius Caesar, prescribed massage as a treatment for many disorders. Galen learned about massage from administering to the health needs of the gladiators and from studying the human body. He believed in the importance of moderation in life, and emphasized the use of massage and hydrotherapy (the use of water to treat diseases or injuries) as a positive part of a balanced life of work, pleasure, sex, alcohol, and exercise. History shows Galen's wise advice fell on deaf ears as the decadent lifestyle of the average Roman contributed more to the corruption and decline of the empire than any warring enemy ever did.

Ah-So! Ancient Cultures of the Far East

The oldest known book about massage was *Cong-Fu of Tao-Tse*, written in China in 3000 C.E. In the 1700s, the book was translated into French. In ancient China the mostly widely used massage of the time was called "Anmo," which literally means "pressing and rubbing." Archeologists have found massage treatments for illnesses inscribed on bones as far back as the Shang Dynasty in the sixteenth through eleventh centuries B.C.E.

Around 1400 B.C.E., the Chinese developed a highly elaborate system that charted the flow of chi (energy) in the body along meridians. Chi travels in the same way neurotransmitters travel along the nerves all through our body. The difference is that meridians are believed to be paths that convey energy and vital force—a system like our nervous system but more delicate and less tangible. The Chinese believed (and many still do) that all illnesses are due to imbalances in the flow of chi. Massage is one of the many techniques the Chinese developed to balance the flow of chi. Chinese massage, called acupressure massage, applies pressure to specific points along the meridians to balance the flow of chi.

The Chinese relied on herbs, acupressure massage, and acupuncture treatments (use of needles on those same acupressure points), to create balance, flow, and wellness.

> ### Goddess Helen Says
>
> There is an old Chinese story dating back to 5000 B.C.E. about a wife who deeply mourned the death of her husband. As was the custom in that day, the body was prepared for burial and, once it was ready, pallbearers carried the body around the outside of the deceased person's home three times. As the pallbearers made their final trip around the house with the woman's husband, they bumped his foot on a corner. Suddenly the husband revived and sat up!
>
> According to the legend, the blow to the foot hit a chi point (which later came to be called Bubbling Spring, also known as Kidney-1) on the sole of the foot. Bumping this point brought the husband out of a deep coma. He survived in good health for another three years, when he died. At the second funeral, the widow implored the pallbearers to be careful not to bump her husband's feet!

The Indians Wrote *the Book* on Love!

The culture in India embraced a new way of looking at intimate relationships, with the publication of the groundbreaking love manual, *The Kama Sutra*, in the third century. The power of the *Kama Sutra of Vatsayama* (Aphorisms on Love) is alive and well today. That famous text for lovemaking, often construed as a spiritual path to ecstasy but foremost a practical guide for living in union with a mate, is still considered one of the best self-help sex guides in the world. From tips on kissing to numerous sexual positions, a constant theme of the book is touch. How to touch, when to touch, where to touch, and how to blend pleasure, love, sensuality, and spirit are the hallmarks of this guide.

Dr. Patti Says

Kama Sutra is the single most widely read guidebook for couples in the world (and it has illustrations that will knock your socks off!). Its very name makes virgins blush. What I particularly love about the *Kama Sutra* approach to intimacy is its emphasis on honoring your partner. How about these amazing guidelines?

- ◆ Take time to know your partner inside and out.
- ◆ Find the ways to ensure your lover's pleasure.
- ◆ Discover the joys of foreplay.
- ◆ Learn the skills to sustain your performance.
- ◆ Delight in the subtle aspects of sensuality and pleasure.

If you search for only one book on lovemaking, make *Kama Sutra* your top pick.

Over time, sensual massage flourished around the world. Imagine, for example, if you could travel back in history to peek into the rooms of a medieval castle. You might see, hear, or smell some wild things behind the velvet drapes. Thinking back to days of chain mail, helmets, armor that dragged you down the stairs from the sheer weight of the suits, all conjure up a nonsensual life. Perhaps, though, behind the massive castle walls, inside some rounded turret, a maiden rub-a-dub-dubbed her princely boyfriend or a guard stole midnight kisses from his sweetheart while caressing the nape of her quivering neck.

Going Swedish: The Story of Peter Ling

Massage started getting some mainstream attention in the West in the late 1700s and early 1800s thanks to a gymnastics instructor from Sweden. Professor Peter Ling, who suffered severe rheumatism, read a French translation of *Cong-Fu of Tao-Tse*, the ancient Chinese text describing massage. Mr. Ling combined his knowledge of physiology, gymnastics, and experiments with the Chinese massage techniques to cure his rheumatism. He called his massage and exercise therapies the Swedish movement system.

Today the Swedish movement system has evolved into Swedish massage. Ling's technique was eventually endorsed by the Swedish government, which conferred it with respectability. A colleague of Mr. Ling, Dr. Johann Mezger, was influential in bringing massage to mainstream physicians as a scientific treatment of pain and disease. The practice became popular in Britain around 1814.

The widely practiced technique includes the following movements:

- **Effleurage.** These are long, gliding, fluid strokes that are sure to make your honey purr.

- **Petrissage.** Pick up the muscles and squeeze, roll, or wring them like kneading dough.

- **Friction or circular rubbing**. The skin will flush, creating heat.

- **Tapotement or percussion.** Practice your drumming skills here with tapping, cupping, and clapping.

- **Vibration or shaking.** A trembling movement that actually feels pretty good.

Mainstreaming Touch: From Europe to the United States

By 1860 Swedish massage had gained a foothold in the United States. The British and French medical establishments helped legitimize Swedish massage in America as a scientific treatment for pain and disease. Doctors began to prescribe massage for illnesses and medical problems of all kinds, including fatigue and tension. People who found comfort and relief from massage began to utilize it for pleasure as well as health. Schools began to train nurses and issue certificates to prove that practitioners were skilled in the arts of the Swedish massage system.

Around 1900, however, the professional massage movement suffered a devastating blow. A report published by the British medical association noted that many schools of massage were issuing false certificates to massage students and sexual impropriety was running rampant in supposedly legitimate massage establishments. Making matters worse, claims of the curative powers of massage were being exaggerated. The American Medical Association denounced massage, paving the way for the advent of wonder drugs that became the focus of mainstream medicine. Although massage continued to be practiced by a few, the general public put their faith in scientists touting pharmacology as the cure for all human ills.

More Than Skin Deep: The Touch Healing Movement

It wasn't until the 1960s that America began to see a revival of massage therapy, with the emergence of the holistic health movement—a movement that's still going strong today. A holistic approach to massage means treating the person as a complete organism, not just alleviating a group of symptoms. The saying that massage is more than skin deep is true. Holistic massage manipulates muscles using a variety of massage techniques to restore circulation, flexibility, and balance of energy as well as to relieve pain and discomfort. As in Chinese massage, the neuromuscular system is calmed and energy is restored. The holistic practitioner must understand anatomy and physiology and also have a feeling (either innate or learned) for life's energy.

You're Putty in My Hands: Spa Time

Spa means "healing waters." In Victorian times in England, around the early 1900s, healing spas were popular for ailments such as rheumatism, arthritis, and similar painful conditions. People would travel to drink and bathe in the famed waters in spas. Spiritual and healing spas really took off in the United States in the 1960s, and since then have become a highlight of pampering, healing, and beauty. Spas are one of the fastest growing industries today—right up there with coffee houses!

Spas can be broken down into three basic categories, as follows:

- ◆ **Day spas.** These have become so popular that unless you live completely out in the sticks, you'll find one. Although day spas started out focusing on healing massage, they have gone far beyond getting rid of that nagging pain in the back. Most now focus on massage for relaxation/pleasure *and* healing. Day spas offer various facial treatments and bodywork treatments, such as deep tissue or Swedish massage.

- ◆ **Resort spas.** These are usually located in quality hotels and offer a large menu of services. Some of these services include the big three of (1) hydrotherapy; (2) thalassotherapy (similar to hydrotherapy with added elements like sea salt, seaweed, and algae, which contain ingredients that help to increase blood circulation, eliminate toxins, and tone and replace minerals in the body); (3) Vichy shower (usually used after other body therapy; a massage therapist lays you on your stomach then shoots alternating jets of pulsating water on your back). Resorts also often offer steam showers, mud wraps, salt scrubs, seaweed treatments, hot stone massage, aromatherapy massage, and/or four hands massage (which is just like it sounds, 'cause you know four hands are better than two!).

Finger Tip

Today's spa devotee is better educated about the mind/body aspect of massage or how it affects them psychologically as well as spiritually.

- ◆ **Stand-alone spas.** These are properties devoted exclusively to the spa experience. They offer full lodging, meals, spa programs, nutritional counselors, and wellness evaluations. Stand-alone spas usually offer specialized treatments, which may include mud or mineral soaks, holistic education, weight loss and management programs, nutritional counseling, and a host of delectable treats for your health, beauty, youthfulness, wellness, and recreational needs. People who attend these spas typically want a life makeover or intense healing experience and are willing to pay big bucks to get it. Massage is always a key element in their programs.

> **Goddess Helen Says**
>
> The International SPA Association (ISPA) defines the spa experience as "your time to relax, reflect, revitalize, and rejoice." It's their objective to revitalize humanity … for a price.

Massage Is Best When East Meets West

The breakthrough of travel and telecommunications opened America to the knowledge of Eastern cultures, especially Indian, Chinese, Indonesian, and Japanese. Some of their energizing systems include the following, based on traditional techniques from the Far East:

- **Thai:** a combination of yoga stretching, twisting, acupressure, and massage (done with clothes on)

- **Shiatsu:** the use of finger pressure on points along meridians of the body to balance and unblock energy (done with clothes on)

- **Lomi Lomi:** an energetic Hawaiian massage method that uses rocking techniques

- **Polarity:** a technique for balancing energy through pressing and holding on different points and parts of the body

- **Reiki:** a form of energy exchange (passed on by a master) that aligns the body energies by placing hands gently on parts of the body in a sequence

- **Watsu:** a gentle underwater massage

- **Reflexology:** a technique involving pressing the feet or hands to bring relief to corresponding parts of the body

With the explosion of Eastern massage ideas and practices in the United States, people began to recognize the Eastern way of understanding the body and the brain as a complete organism—rather than two separate entities—that should be treated accordingly.

> **Goddess Helen Says**
>
> Most massage therapists, including myself, do eclectic massage. I start out with some long, sensual Swedish strokes to relax and soothe the body. But when I find a tight muscle, you'd better believe that I switch to a more intense style or even some acupressure to release the tightness, along with encouraging the recipient to do some deep breathing. What an amazing experience it can be to savor different strokes and techniques blended from all areas of the world and from all eras of time. I love that part of my work!

Now people have access to many more forms of healing massage and sensuality.

Your head is probably spinning from tracing the evolution of massage over time and around the world. Remnants of ancient techniques are alive today in the many styles and approaches for healing touch. But touch is more than just a way to heal disease, overcome your aches and pains, or feel renewed. Touch is the big picture of which sensual massage is a part of.

The Least You Need to Know

- ◆ Massage techniques are as old as human existence.

- ◆ The Swedish massage system draws from ancient Chinese sources and modern physiological knowledge.

- ◆ Chinese and other Eastern massage techniques focus on balancing the flow of the body's energy.

- ◆ Massage can provide a range of healthful benefits, from improved circulation to pain management.

- ◆ Massage today has taken on many forms and techniques.

The Continuum of Touch

In This Chapter

- The different kinds of touch
- Strokes that feel good
- Intimate strokes
- The fine line between sensual and sexual touch

The touch techniques you use should be dictated only by the limits of your imagination (okay, okay, we also believe that the techniques you use should never harm you or your partner). But before you can let your imagination run wild, you need to know what kinds of massage touches there are. And while all massage can be pleasurable, sensual massage differs from other kinds not so much in the types of techniques used, but in its purpose: It's meant to evoke *sensual* pleasure and even sexuality. That's one road that most professional massages better not take you down!

In this chapter, we'll look at massage as a part of the touch continuum—that line of touch from the healing techniques of a professional to the kinds of touch that can produce heights of ecstasy, and eventually, should you choose to go that far, orgasmic bliss.

Once you're familiar with all parts of the touch continuum, you'll be ready to choose the kind of touch that you want to engage in each time you share a massage.

The Balance Beam: From Sensual to Sexual and Beyond

The continuum of sensual touch moves from lesser to greater levels of intimacy and personal exposure. Let's take a look at the continuum of touch and where sensual massage fits in.

| Healing | Affection | Sensual | Erotic | Sexual |

- **Healing:** This is the kind of touch that you might pay massage therapists for. You can also receive healing touch from a friend who does this for his or her own gratification or maybe from a nurse during a hospital stay. Even your honey can administer healing touch if he's savvy about what he's doing or has taken a course on how to channel healing energy with his hands. Often, healing touch is the kind you want when you are sick, tired, or in pain.

- **Affection:** On this part of the continuum, touch is used to show friendship, caring, and nurturance. It can even be a "Glad to see you, Frankie" kind of gesture—a hand on the shoulder or arm. Think guys patting each other's butts on a football field as a sign of affection, support, and encouragement. The touch is playful, light, or silly.

- **Sensual:** Sensual touch is touch for the pleasure it gives—lavishing in touch for its own sake or to bring two people closer together. Sensual touch can lead to the next two levels of touch along the continuum, should you decide to take it that far.

- **Erotic:** Erotic touch is usually associated with good old foreplay to sex—it's those kinds of intimate touches, such as deep kissing or petting that often lead to sexual intercourse.

> **Dr. Patti Says**
>
> Foreplay can happen at any point along the continuum, with or without erotic touch.

- **Sexual:** Sexual touch can be as simple as kissing, but also can involve anything two naked bodies might do together, including petting, oral-genital contact, penile-vaginal intercourse, G-spot stimulation, anal sex, or whatever else you can dream of. Using your bodies—including your genitals—for sexual pleasure is what distinguishes sexual touch from others kinds of touch.

You and your partner should talk about the kind of touch you wish to give and receive *before* you begin the massage. That way, there will be no hurt feelings or dashed hopes.

Goddess Helen Says

If you're looking for a healing massage rather than a sensual massage, it's best to seek professional help. One of the best ways to get a referral for a massage therapist is through a friend. Your health insurance may even cover massage therapy—ask. Often massage therapists have their own office and advertise through their associations. Two such association are the Associated Bodywork and Massage Professionals and the International Massage Association. Or try searching online for a therapist in your area.

It Takes Two to Tango: Sensual Massage for Pleasure

Now it's time to take a look at some strokes that are designed for your pleasure. Try these on for size:

- Long slow strokes over the skin
- Deep, probing strokes on the shoulders, legs, and arms
- Light little finger kisses that ignite sensation
- Softly gliding the palm of your hand over the whole body
- Gently pulling fingers through the hair
- Sucking the toes
- Giving a nice back rub or tummy rub

To make your touch time more pleasurable, try slowing down and using a lighter touch.

Wondering which strokes go with healing, pleasure, erotic, or sexual touch? Well, maybe the following examples will help.

For healing, you may find that you feel more confident or even do a better job at pushing deeply into the tissues, making you more of a deep tissue massage giver; or you might like the long slow strokes on the surface of the skin that are the mark of the Swedish method. Then again, you may feel like learning more on your own about acupressure and become a savvy points-pusher.

For pleasure, you might develop a combination of strokes, rhythms, and intensities or special movements. These will probably change with time and as you develop your own unique style. Maybe you like to make little butterfly wings with your fingers on your partner's flesh or pull on your lover's earlobes, or even use your mouth more than your fingers as your style. The whole idea is to create sensations that feel good to the receiver.

To get more erotic, focus on the sensual parts of the body, such as the buttocks, the chest, the inner thigh or around the sides of the neck. In Chapter 18, we will guide you into the pleasurable erogenous zones, to give you a good idea of where the good-ies can be found.

For sexual touch, it's pretty obvious that if you include the breasts and the genitals in your touch treatment, you will probably get the kind of response you're looking for! Use your creativity to discover what may be a sizzling move on your part. Speeding up, pushing more intensely, moving your fingers in different patterns, even using more than your hand, such as your tongue or a toy, may be just what the doctor ordered!

One of the best benefits of sensual massage is pleasure. Pleasure, simply put, is what feels good. You may find pleasure in petting your new puppy's soft fur, watching that fuchsia-and-gold sunset over a Maui horizon, or winning the lottery. Oh, and let's not forget about the pleasure of feeling loved.

Dr. Patti Says

Dr. Harry Harlow (1905–1981) was a psychologist who specialized in primate studies and whose life's work was the study of love. In Harlow's studies of rhesus monkeys in the 1950s, he found that those monkey babies who were nursed using a wire "mother" were less affectionate than those nursed by a cloth "mother." Touch and early affection were the factors that influenced their differences. Even a banana-munching chimp got more than just bottled milk from leaning up against a figure covered in fabric!

Harlow's research shows us that even at its most primal, touch can feel good. From cradle to grave, humans need to touch and be touched.

Touch goes both ways, too—through giving *and* receiving. It doesn't take much to bring you into that realm of "feel good" stuff. Even the slightest level or amount of skin-to-skin contact makes a difference in gratifying the basic human need for touch.

You Turn Me on Like a Radio: Sensual Massage as Foreplay for Sex

It can be misleading to think that foreplay is all about the body. It's not. Foreplay can happen between the ears just as easily as between the sheets or the thighs. But once you add sensual massage to your sexual repertoire, you are likely to take off like a missile into outer space.

Contemplate what you are interested in having as foreplay for a sexual interlude before it happens. For example, you may like to hear romantic music or the sounds of breathing to get you in the mood. Or maybe you need visual cues, such as seeing your honey in lacy lingerie (or bikini briefs) standing at the doorway. Whatever it is that gets your motor running to kick start the process for sensual massage, discover what works for you. Then share that with the lucky person you are about to touch.

Getting into touch early on in the process and focusing on sensual massage may be the beginning of a long night of sexual pleasure.

Here are some ways to use sensual massage for foreplay:

- ◆ Warm oils on the skin. More than just the surface of the skin will heat up!

- ◆ Touching the obvious places, such as lips on lips, the nipples, the groin, genitals, and buttocks can send the perfect message that it's time for nookie.

- ◆ Slow, deliberate strokes will help to kindle the fire.

- ◆ Using parts of *your* body as the massage tool or toy, such as your hair, your tongue, your breast or breath, will send him into ecstatic realms. Your foreplay with this kind of sensual massage may last a nano-second before sex starts!

There's no doubt about it: A good sensual massage can serve as foreplay to sex, helping you along the way to a good orgasm.

Gene and Trista are ready for action—skin to skin. The heat of the fire behind them is nothing compared to what they feel.

(Robert Dunlap)

Couples often report that they don't have an easy time getting into a satisfying sexual experience with their lover. What does that mean? Sex is much more than a mechanical act and it's also more than just sexual intercourse (penis-in-vagina sex) or the "main entrée" in the sexual act. What couples often lack are the skills for foreplay. That's where sensual massage comes in.

Couples spend about 80 percent of a sexual act approaching their climax, 5 to 10 percent in it, and the rest of their time (10 to 15 percent) in what we like to call the "afterglow." For some couples, the touch that precedes the main entrée, or the hors d'oeuvres part of their encounter, includes a hearty serving of sensual massage. The same applies to the afterglow period, when couples often feel the urge to bond. At those times sensual massage may be the perfect way to stay connected, feel the closeness, and allow the wonderful feelings of letting go continue as you give and receive sensual touch. (In Chapter 18, we talk more about foreplay. There we'll give you ideas for incorporating sensual massage into your lovemaking experience. So hang in there!)

Finger Tip

Did you know that at orgasm both men and women release the hormone oxytocin, which is the same chemical in breastfeeding that creates that mother-infant bond, and which propels those natural feelings of nurturing, bonding, and intimacy?

Dr. Patti Says

I once worked with a sweet couple, married over 20 years and totally devoted to each other. They had everything going for them, their son had moved off to college, and they were rediscovering each other. They seemed like innocent children, as they talked about falling in love again. Sex was a "Slam, bam thank you ma'am" kind of thing, lasting about five minutes, with her not being satisfied and his losing it quickly. They came to me in despair about it, having forgotten the missing ingredient of a good sex life— foreplay. We discussed how adding sensual massage as foreplay could rekindle their lovemaking style. After a month of practice, they had extended their times in bed to more than an hour, found new joys in sensual pleasure, and both lasted to the finish line during sex. Incorporating foreplay skills with sensual massage was their saving grace.

Teaser or Please-er: Sensual vs. Sexual Massage

While a sensual massage certainly can lead to sex, it *doesn't have to*. It can be all about feeling good, without sex entering the picture. You get to choose.

One of the pitfalls of doing sensual massage when you don't want sex is that one or both partners may begin to experience and show signs of sexual arousal, such as an erection, flushed skin, and heavy breathing. Just because the signs of arousal are there, however, doesn't mean that you have to leap into action. In other words, sex as a goal is fine, but sex doesn't have to be the goal of sensual massage. Sometimes all the good intentions to keep the massage sensual (not sexual) can go out the window in a moment of pleasure-giving touch. That's okay, as long as you make the decision together. Be as awake, alert, alive, and present as possible for what's in store for you with this or any other shared bodily pleasure path.

You can use sensual massage as a prelude to a wild bout in the bed, but if you want to enjoy the ride of touch for pleasure and/or healing on its own terms, then say so. Just be sure to make up your mind before you apply the oils to your fingertips and lay his or her body down.

Remember that you are in control of each sensual massage. Be sure to negotiate with your partner about whether or not you want to act on your sexual arousal.

 Ouch!

Be clear about your intentions. If you are really looking for sex, then you can easily use sensual massage as a luxurious foreplay experience. If, on the other hand, you want to have time for just sharing the senses and getting closer without sexual contact, express your desires with your partner beforehand.

Goddess Helen Says

Couples are often surprised to find that sensual massage evokes the awakening of their senses, creates intimacy without sex as the goal, and can be a spiritual ritual. One couple I taught discovered that their sensual massage time became their spiritual practice each week. The sheer fact of holding each other, taking time to stop the frantic pace of life, and extend love to one another changed their relationship for the better. And their health improved to boot!

The Least You Need to Know

◆ Touch is a basic human need.

◆ Hands-on touch can be healing all by itself.

◆ Sensual touch may be the perfect foreplay.

◆ Be sure to discuss with your partner whether your sensual massage will lead to sexual play.

3

Stroking Your Way to Health

In This Chapter

- ◆ How massage helps your health
- ◆ Fighting fatigue and stress
- ◆ Improving circulation, immunity, and oxygenation
- ◆ Giving your mood a boost

There aren't enough things we do in life that feel good and are good for us—but sensual massage definitely tops this list! In addition to making us feel great, sensual massage—like any kind of massage—has oodles of positive health benefits. Tiredness, negative stressors, lack of proper breathing, dead skin cells, puffy tissue, a poor immune system, and your outlook on life can all be helped with a little tender touch. Although we know that you aren't stroking your honey for health, you should still know what good things those strokes can do for you—both physically and mentally.

A Touch a Day Keeps the Doctor Away

The whole idea behind new age holistic cures—herbal remedies, yoga, acupuncture, meditation, and so on—is that your body has the amazing ability to heal itself. Massage, too, can be used to help your body's own healing abilities.

Ouch!

We are always surprised by how many people think that massages are only for the rich. Wrong! The average price for a massage is between $45 to $80 per hour. Still think your budget's too tight? The cost to treat yourself to a luxurious rejuvenating massage is probably less than a month's worth of those designer coffees you rely on for your wake-up call.

Goddess Helen Says

There is a secret communication that occurs between the person giving and the person receiving the massage. To trained fingers, for instance, tight muscles feel differently than relaxed muscles do. It takes time and patience to learn this subtle language, but by explaining how massage therapy works, you'll start to get a feel for what we mean.

Getting Under Your Partner's Skin

When you rub muscles, beneath the surface of your partner's skin, your massage is improving blood flow. This gets fluids moving more efficiently, thereby cleansing the body of bacteria and waste. So in a way your massage is not only calming your partner or giving him pleasure, but also taking out his or her metabolic garbage. Aside from getting sick, not taking out the body's waste products makes people lethargic and depletes them of energy.

Finger Tip

Do you want to send your partner a massage valentine that will bond the two of you? Bend a leg up to the ceiling by lifting up the foot. Now let that lifted foot lean against your chest or abdomen. Put both of your hands around your partner's ankle like a human ankle bracelet. Applying pressure slowly, slide your hands up your partner's leg toward the knee. This massage movement will increase and propel blood flow toward the heart, without putting additional strain on it. You can do the same thing to your partner's arms, starting from the wrist and moving to the elbow. What a great way to heal an achy heart!

Fatigue Fighter

When you're worried and stressed, chances are your body is secreting the stress hormone cortisol. This hormone prepares your body for a flight-or-fight response, which is fine if you're under attack but not if you want to relax and get a great night's sleep.

One beautiful remedy for fatigue is right there at your fingertips—massage. When you receive a massage, pain blocking hormones such as enkephalin and endorphins (the "feel good" hormones) are released. These counteract or block the effects of cortisol, allowing you to melt into rest and sleep like a baby.

Now that you know that massage is a great remedy for your fatigue, don't start a fight over who's going to get the first massage or you'll get the cortisol pumping again. We know you'll figure it out, and you'll both sleep much better for having relieved your anxiety and tension. And while you're sleeping your amazing body will regenerate itself.

Finger Tip

If your partner has been suffering from insomnia, give him a massage in the evening. That way he can roll into bed and sleep the night away. Give your partner at least a half-hour massage, as it may take the body that long to de-stress. If you receive a massage in the afternoon, rest easy—a one-hour massage can be the equivalent of two or three hours of sleep.

Stress Buster

Stress causes a release of hormones that make the blood vessels narrow and constrict, which means less blood flow. This, in turn, will cause your heart to work harder and your breathing to become rapid and shallow. Digestion slows down. In fact all body processes begin to experience dysfunction. Symptoms of stress include headaches, hypertension, depression, low back pain, and insomnia. An estimated 80 to 90 percent of illnesses are stress induced.

Let's look at some of the common stress factors in our lives.

- Divorce/the end of a long-term relationship

- Unemployment or problems at work

- Pregnancy/childbirth/starting a family

- Moving

- Financial problems and serious debt

- Lack of love or support

- Family problems

- Sexual dysfunction or repressed sexual desires

We all have our unique stressors, and we handle stress in an amazing variety of ways. Sensual massage, however, seems to be a universal remedy for stress.

During a massage, your muscles relax. Your heart rate slows down, allowing a release of tension, and your breathing deepens. All of this increases the blood flow to the muscles and eliminates toxins, which have built up as a result of stress. Sensual massage is the best nonprescription drug for healing stress-related diseases.

Stress has the power to destroy relationships, but sensual massage is a great way to overcome that stress and bring couples together. One couple we know have been giving each other massages every week for six years now. They integrate massage into their lives and use it for their stress management. They hire a sitter to look after their children (two boys under the age of six). They think of their massage date as an investment in their health—it gives them time to focus on themselves and to connect with each other. Even if you become "addicted" to massaging each other, would that be such a bad thing?

The River of Life: Circulation

The circulation of blood throughout the body is essential to healthy sexuality. It is blood moving into and through the sexual organs that produces erections, thereby arousing both males and females. Without that blood flow, you probably wouldn't have the capacity for being sexual at all. A good sensual massage, with its circulatory benefits, can help that blood move freely. Not only does good circulation help with sex, it is the basis for all good health.

Power Boost: Improving the Immune Response

Your lymphatic system is responsible for your body's ability to ward off infections and heal injuries. The lymphatic system doesn't have a pump of its own like the blood system. Instead, it is dependent on the contraction and massaging of muscles to keep the lymph moving freely around the body. It's the lymph that aids in the production of white blood cells, which in turn strengthens the immune system to help fight infections. If you don't have an active lifestyle, chances are your lymphatic system is sluggish.

Studies undertaken by the Touch Research Institute in Miami found that people who received massages had higher levels of infection-fighting white blood cells. These touched bodies also showed an increased activity of so-called "natural killer cells" that attack disease.

Now you know why you have been getting those recurring colds! Never mind that flu shot. Instead you may want to give your system a boost with a sensual massage.

> **CAUTION**
>
> **Ouch!**
>
> Lymphatic tissue is found in concentrated areas of the body, such as the armpit, groin, neck, knees, stomach and in the chest. These are called lymph nodes and they are responsible for filtering bacteria and preventing it from entering the bloodstream. If any of these areas are swollen on your partner, or if they are painful, do not massage them, as this could increase the swelling. If in doubt check it out with your doctor.

Fill 'Er Up: Oxygenation

Like a squeezed sponge, a tight muscle can't hold much fluid nor can it allow fluid to pass through it. This decreases circulation and increases the strain on your heart, robbing it of precious energy.

Massage relaxes contracted muscles and helps the circulation by pushing blood toward the heart, therefore relieving strain on this vital organ. Think of the strain of a bottleneck traffic jam—traffic simply gets stuck and can't move. Your body works the same way. An increase of circulation brings energy-producing nutrients and oxygen to your cells while carrying away metabolic waste products that make you feel listless and drained.

Ready for another bonus from your sensual massage session? Massage will increase the body's oxygen-carrying cell count, namely hemoglobin, which will help to bring more oxygen to your body's cells.

Injured muscles heal faster with massage. More and more, science is making the discovery that degenerative diseases like cancer and muscular sclerosis are anaerobic. They simply cannot

> **Finger Tip**
>
> The circulatory system is run by the heart. It transports about 10.5 pints of blood per minute when the body is resting and it pumps up to an amazing 42 pints during strenuous exercise. The adult body contains about 12 pints of blood. That means that even when you are resting, all of your blood makes a complete circulation in just over a minute. Massage alone increases the blood capacity by at least 10 to 15 percent.

survive in an oxygenated environment. You may find that through sensual massage by itself you have more energy, look more vibrant, feel better all over, and fend off infections more easily. So what are you waiting for?

Shaping Up

In a perfect world, we would work out three times a week! But that's probably the last thing on your mind after a long day at work. And you know how sore your muscles get when you haven't worked out for a while. It's lactic acid that makes your muscles sore, and massage removes lactic acid by increasing blood circulation. Your sensual massage also will increase muscle flexibility and range of motion. Now you can get into those Kama Sutra positions you've been trying to figure out!

And if you're embarrassed about cellulite, massage along with diet and exercise can result in smoother skin. Massage and exercise together purify the body, increasing circulation and muscle tone.

Real Skinny on Skin

Your skin has two distinct layers: the upper layer is the epidermis, and the lower layer, under the epidermis, is the dermis. The dermis contains sweat glands, nerve endings, sensors for touch, hair follicles, and countless capillaries that supply the nutritional needs of the cells of the skin. The epidermis has no direct blood supply; it produces the hair and nails, protects and waterproofs you, and manufactures new skin cells. The skin keeps toxins out, blood in, and the body cool.

The dermal layer contains five separate sensors that detect heat, cold, pressure, pain, and light or ticklish touch. That's why a sensual massage on the skin creates so many sensations—from tickle to ahhhhhhhhhhh.

We all know that too much sun, smog, or unhealthy food accelerates the visible signs of aging, such as dry and wrinkled skin. But did you know that massage brings more blood to the skin, resulting in a more youthful glow? With every massage stroke, you are removing toxins from the blood and delivering vital nutrients to the skin. Massage also helps reduce itchy skin by improving the function of the sebaceous gland, which lubricates and protects it from infection. Plus, a good old rubbing will accelerate the sweat glands that cool and clean the skin. As you apply oils with your sensual massage, you will be getting a dual effect, moisturizing from the outside in and the inside out.

Goddess Helen Says

Your skin plays an important role in your life—not just for sensual massage, but for your beauty, your health, and your whole being. Your skin requires TLC. Tender, loving care goes a long way in helping your skin thrive and glow.

Three wonderful things you can do for your skin are as follows:

- **Brush the skin.** Use a skin brush on dry skin before you shower or bathe. Exfoliate it on a regular basis. Daily brushing away the dead skin cells that collect on the surface will restore its healthy glow.

- **Moisturize the skin.** Use selected oils, lotions, and soaps. Avoid soaps that are detergent or that contain antimicrobial properties, as they deplete your skin of its natural protective functions. Any time you receive a sensual massage with oils, you are feeding your skin.

- **Drink for the skin.** The human body is comprised of more than 60 percent water. Most Westerners consume far less water than they need. Water regulates your body temperature through sweating and exhalation from the lungs. Drink 8 glasses of water and your skin will show it. No more sagging, dried out, or pinched look on those shins or upper arms!

It's All in Your Head: Mental Health

How you feel emotionally and mentally has a major bearing on your physical health and well-being. Some of the leading psychologists suggest that you are what you think and feel. We agree! For example, if you have just had a fight with your oldest child about homework or found out that your business partner lied to you, you are not going to feel well. You may have tightness in your chest, a stomachache, or non-specific pain somewhere in your body that you cannot attribute to an injury or over-doing it at the gym. But massage has the amazing ability to change your mood and your entire outlook on life. It can give your attitude a boost when you're feeling down in the dumps, and it can turn an already good day into a great one! Isn't that reason enough to keep on reading?

The Least You Need to Know

- Sensual massage can de-stress you.

- Studies show that massage contributes to better functioning of the immune system.

- Massage can make your skin healthier.

- A good massage can improve your mood.

Chapter 4

Tools of the Trade

In This Chapter

- ◆ Choosing which oils work best
- ◆ Different textures for different sensations
- ◆ Pillows for proper positioning
- ◆ Playing around with massage toys

This chapter is going to cover the basics and then some. All the things that you will need to put in your massage treasure trove to be sure that when it's time to touch, you have what we consider to be the necessary (and not-so-necessary) accessories. Of course, we all know that you could just set up a corner of the living room, lay your honey down on her tummy, remove her top, and start pushing her flesh. But if you want to maximize your sensual massage experience, read on.

The line of necessities for a successful sensual massage often includes oils, something to lie on, textured cloths, and pleasure toys. Why? Part of the process of sensual massage is about awakening the senses and opening the gateway for pleasure.

Lubing Up

The first massage essential that you'll need to get your hands on is some sort of lubricant. You're going to need something between your hands and your partner's body that allows your hands to glide over the skin with smooth, sensual movements.

Although you could certainly use lotion for massage, we have found that it absorbs into the skin far too quickly. Instead of enjoying the process of extending pleasure, you'll be cursing under your breath as you apply more and more lotion.

Ouch!

Make sure that neither you nor your partner is allergic to any oils, especially peanuts or avocado, or to any of the ingredients in a massage oil mixture, such as chemicals or perfume. When in doubt, test it out. Rub a tiny bit of oil (or lotion) on your wrist and keep it on without washing for 24 hours. If irritation or a breakout occurs on the skin, don't use that particular oil.

Finger Tip

Oil feels best if it's warmer than your body temperature. Place your bottle of oil in a pot of warm water for approximately 20 minutes to warm it up. Or splurge and buy yourself a commercial oil warmer. If your room temperature is steamy and sultry already, cut back your warm up time to 10 minutes. Warm oil is easier to apply and feels good to both giver and receiver.

Carrier Oils

Unlike lotion, oil will last longer, and we consider it to be the ideal choice for massage.

Every massage movement is easier with oil that allows the hands to glide, nourishes the skin, and arouses the senses. Ready-made massage oils can be purchased at health food stores, or you can get inventive. Look around your kitchen for vegetable oils such as sunflower, peanut, or safflower oils, all of which are excellent for massage and are called "carrier oils."

Other carrier oils that you might consider include the following:

- **Coconut oil:** It can be purchased in economical tubs (in solid form; it liquefies at room temperature) at health food stores, and unlike most other oils or lotions, is absorbed into the skin after gentle heating. It's like food for your skin.

- **Apricot kernel oil:** An odorless pale yellow oil that contains minerals and vitamins and can be applied to all types of skin. This oil is very helpful to prematurely aging skin, and dry, inflamed or sensitive skin.

- **Avocado oil:** Dark green in color, this carrier oil comes from the fruit itself. It contains protein, vitamins, fatty acids, lecithin, and it is odorless. Great for all skin types, especially if you have eczema or dry skin.

- **Grape seed oil** (Helen's personal choice): We recommend this oil for all types of skin. It is almost colorless and contains minerals, proteins, and vitamins. Helen likes it because it's so light.

- **Jojoba** (this one's a little pricey): This yellow oil comes from the jojoba bean. Because it is slightly thicker than the other oils we have described in this chapter, dilute it 10 percent with a lighter oil, such as grape seed oil. It's excellent for treating psoriasis, acne, eczema, and inflamed skin.

- **Sweet almond oil:** Mmm. And you thought this was a food! It is very pale yellow color, contains minerals, vitamins, and is rich in proteins. It comes from the kernel of the almond and helps relieve itching, soreness, inflammation, and dryness.

- **Wheat germ oil:** It is a yellow-orange color and needs to be diluted 10 percent with a lighter oil, such as sweet almond or grape seed oil. It contains vitamins, minerals, and proteins and is used especially for prematurely aging skin, psoriasis, and eczema, although it is suitable for all skin types.

- **Vitamin E:** Although it's very thick and extremely expensive, vitamin E is great to use on your or your partner's face, which is more delicate than the rest of the skin and requires only a thin coating of oil.

Once you've found a carrier oil that you like working with, you can add an essential oil to it, the fragrance of which will spice up your sensual massage. Mixing essential oils with carrier oils can create different effects on your partner, from relaxing to invigorating, depending on the combination. We discuss essential oils in detail in Chapter 13.

The quantity of oil you use is important. If you add too much oil, your hands will skid all over your partner's body and you will be unable to make proper contact—too little oil and you will end up making uneven, jerky movements.

To aid in getting just the right amount of oil, pour your massage oil into a plastic squeeze

Ouch!
Putting oil of any kind on the face can result in acne or other eruptions or irritations on the skin. Helen recommends using apricot kernel or sweet almond oil on the face, as they are evenly balanced, which is important, as the skin on the face is usually a combination of dry, oily, and normal skin types.

Ouch!
If you are worried about staining sheets or clothes with massage oil, you can purchase nonstaining massage lotions and oils that the professionals use. These are available at massage supply stores.

bottle. When you're ready to begin the massage, pour just enough oil to cover the hollow of your palm. You can always add more if you feel the skin drying out. It is always easier to add more than to mop up too much. Don't add oil to the whole body at once—you can add oil to other parts of the body as you progress.

You can use any of the above-mentioned carrier oils for the feet. However, go lightly with oils on the soles of the feet, so that the person receiving the massage doesn't slip when he gets up to walk and to minimize carpet stains.

Powders

If you or your partner just don't like the feel of oil (or lotion) on your skin or if you are allergic to it, you can use powder to help reduce the friction between the hands and the body. However, we don't recommend that you use talcum powder, as it has been found to cause cervical cancer in women.

We like Kama Sutra honey dust powder, which you brush on with a fun duster. It not only comes in a gorgeous container, but it also smells like Parisian perfume and is edible. Ooh la la!

Every couple needs to brush a little Kama Sutra powder on themselves now and then to tickle their fancy—and it's even edible!

(Robert Dunlap)

There are many natural alternatives to talc, including some that you can make your-self. Here's a recipe for a safe, natural powder that you can have fun with, using a brush for effect:

2 cups cornstarch

1 cup rice flour

Pinch or two powdered herbs (or rose petals or even 2 or 3 vanilla beans) for fragrance

Mix ingredients in an airtight container and leave for a week, adding in one of the suggested fragrances. Transfer into a container of your choice and brush onto your skin with a powder puff or a sable brush.

When applying massage powder with a brush, don't forget those parts of his body that don't get touched much. The feel of the brush can create great sensations all on its own!

> CAUTION
>
> **Ouch!**
> Your skin is your largest organ, so remember wherever you put on oil, it gets absorbed into your blood system. Any petroleum-based oils can be hazardous to the vaginal lining or break down latex condoms. Too much oil of any kind in the vaginal area can lead to a vaginal irritation.

Cleanup Gear

You've surrendered to the moment, and the sensuality is flowing, but so is the fragrant massage oil, which you spilled … oops! It's always a good idea keep a few extra towels on hand to mop up any spills.

If you're planning to give your sweetie a massage on that beautiful down comforter, cover it with another sheet, preferably an old one that you don't mind getting soiled or stained. Lighter colors and patterns camouflage oil stains better than darker colors. Or you could use a plastic sheet under an old sheet, although be aware that using a plastic sheet will create more heat. Unless you are building a bonfire for romance, that type of heat can make you sweat, which may not be what you had in mind.

Knock Me Over with a Feather: Fabrics and Textures

Oils, lotions, and powders create texture between your hand and your partner's skin. The main reason for these massage helpers is to allow you to slip, slide, and glide. And while there's nothing as fine as skin on skin, sometimes using texture beyond your finger pad and a little oil on an aching shoulder, tight buns, or a soft cheek will create pleasure for both the giver and receiver.

Consider using textures for caressing, rubbing, tickling, dragging across a body, or pressing into flesh. Who knows—it just might earn you an encore request. Try one or more of these textured objects when you are ready to begin your actual hands-on session:

- Bath scrubby
- Loofah sponge
- Natural sea sponge (wet or dry)
- Ice cubes
- Pudding (warm, not hot or cold)
- Jell-O (chilled)
- Feathers (peacock plumes, ostrich boas)
- Dried, fresh, or silk flowers
- Cat o' nine tails (leather or nylon)
- Hairbrush (boar's bristle, nylon, or rubber tipped)
- Spoons
- Other textured objects

Some fabrics to consider include the following:

- Velvet or velveteen
- Satin
- Nylon
- Leather or suede
- Cotton plush
- Fake fur
- Silk
- Tulle or organza
- Wide-wale corduroy
- Cashmere wool

Experiment with what feels good. Drag or tease with the object, especially on the back, the legs, the inner thighs, the stomach, or the shoulders to create new and different sensations.

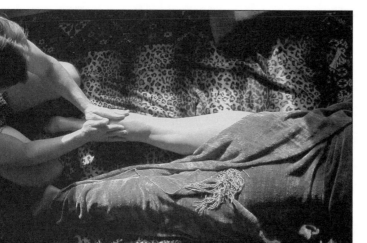

Get creative, like this couple who have chosen to do their sensual massage on a leopard throw with a chenille spread on top to keep her toasty while he does his handiwork.

(Robert Dunlap)

More Cushion for the Pushin'

The first place most people think to give a massage is on their bed. However, most mattresses are too soft and pliable, not offering any support for the giver. For a sensual massage you'll need a firm, strong surface that will support you and your partner.

Before you decide on the kitchen table or the coffee table, assess their stability. If you have extra thick padding under your carpet, then a duvet (essentially, a comforter) on the floor covered with a sheet could do the trick. Giving a massage while kneeling on the floor may cramp your legs, so be sure to place a pillow behind your knees and keep moving around to keep the blood circulating. A double-size futon mattress will also work, but of course there has to be enough room for the person giving the massage to move around.

The most comfortable massage surface for both giver and receiver is one that is firm but has a pliant surface. It supports the back nicely and

CAUTION

Ouch!

Be wise about what you use for your massage platform. Avoid accidental injuries by using stable flooring, tables, or a couch, but don't take chances with anything that may wobble and break. The sheer weight of your body and the added pressure of the massage itself can be too much strain for many tables. As with anything that you choose for pleasure, always put safety first!

doesn't rock or sway when pressure is applied on the body. The best type of surface allows room to move around the massage area, plus has a well-padded surface for knees.

Finger Tip

If you use a table, make sure it isn't too low so that the partner giving the massage doesn't have to hunch over. If the table is too high, you won't be able to apply enough pressure with your body, and believe us when we tell you that you are going to tire easily when only using pressure from your hands. Being at just the right height will propel you into lasting action.

Determining the appropriate height for your massage surface is simple. Stand next to the table with your arms down by your side and make a fist. If your fist is level with the surface, then it's just right. If it's not, then you need to adjust the height.

Going Pro

If you find that you really like giving and receiving sensual massages, you may want to go all out and invest in a professional massage table. Expect to pay around $250 for a basic table with adjustable legs and a face cradle, which is a donut-shaped extension of the table where the receiver's head rests. We recommend the fine tables from Living Earth Crafts, Earthlite, and Oakworks. They all come with a manufacturer's guarantee and you can buy them in massage supply stores. You can even buy a carrying case if you plan on taking your table on that Hawaiian vacation.

Not only does a massage table enable you to massage while standing up (which is less tiring than kneeling), your partner will also be more comfortable with her head cradled in that funny donut hole. Single (twin) sheets fit most massage tables. When you're not using the table, you can fold it up and stash it under the bed or in the closet. Pretty neat, eh?

Dr. Patti Says

Liberator Shapes come in four dandy geometrical shapes for propping you up for sensual and sexual pleasure. The Cube, Ramp, Wedge, and Stage are large platforms made of durable hard foam, with multiple layers of covers of washable velvety cotton and nylon, all in sassy colors! Shapes allow for new angles and creative positioning, comfort, building stamina, and reaching tight or inaccessible parts of the body with greater ease. See our Resources List in the Appendix for where to find them.

Bigger Joys with Bigger Toys

It seems that no matter how old we get, we still like to play with toys. Discovering the joy of massage toys is fun! Consider trying one or more of these four basic types of massage tools and toys:

- **Pressure point toys:** If you have ever used your thumb to press on your partner's tight shoulder muscles, you probably noticed that your thumb got tired very quickly. Pressure point toys, which look like knobs, will not only relieve your partner of her pain but also take strain off your hands and thumbs.

- **Roller toys:** Roller-type massage toys feel incredible on the bottom of the feet, but they can be used on other parts of the body, too. Stick to those body parts with thick muscles and plenty of flesh, like the buttocks and the upper back. Or try using a tennis ball under your fingers and the palm of your hands.

- **Vibrating toys:** Oh yes! As your partner massages your body with vibration massage toys, all your *meridians* are stimulated. Get yourself one of those big shoulder massage power tools—the one- or two-headed plug-in monsters with rotating heads. (Panasonic and Hitachi make wonderful wands.) Use it on large muscles—not delicate parts. Or consider buying a ring massager that fits on your finger, vibrating claws that simulate a four-finger massage, or even some of the battery-operated goodies.

- **Claw toys.** These little toys have a ball that you grasp in your palm. On the other side of the ball are three extensions that you can use to massage your partner. Think of these extensions as extra fingers pressing down simultaneously and with

Finger Tip

Variety may be the spice of life, but it's not the main course. If the whole point of sensual massage is for the two of you to touch each other, then the massage is your main course. Massage toys are the natural offshoots of that, or the spice.

Touch Term

Meridians are energy paths in our bodies that convey vital force or chi. There are 26 main meridian paths (12 pairs on either side of the body and 2 single paths).

Ouch!

While massage toys feel great on fleshy and muscular parts of the body, they are not designed for massaging over bone. Avoid using them on the spine and bony areas like ribs, elbows, and knees.

equal pressure. This feels great on the shoulders and in between the shoulder blades. It can also be used for tickling and scratching.

Kevin and Martha Ellen are playing with Nukkles massage toys for kneading tight muscles and a roller toy for added pleasure.

(Robert Dunlap)

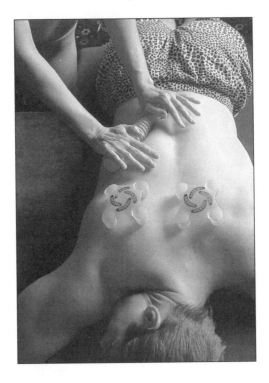

In addition, you might want to keep some squeeze balls for your hands nearby to relieve tension and strengthen the hands.

All the great gadgets and toys will enhance your sensual massage pleasures, but they will never replace your hands and the art of sensual touch. Touch, after all, is what keeps us human.

The Least You Need to Know

- ◆ Oil is the best massage lubricant, but be careful of spills.
- ◆ Your massage surface should be stable and comfortable.
- ◆ Textured objects and fabrics can enhance the pleasure of touch.
- ◆ Don't be afraid to try massage toys.

Part 2

Let's Touch!

We know you're eager to put fingers to skin, so grab a bottle of oil, turn up the temperature, and get ready for your rubdown! This part of the book takes you through all the touch techniques you'll need to turn your partner into a cooing puddle of flesh. You'll learn the basic massage strokes and how to position your body so that you avoid strain and maximize your energy. Whether you want to use your hands, elbows, chin, or cheeks (either kind!), we'll have you rub-a-dub-dubbing in no time.

Although we encourage you to let your intuition be your guide, we break the body down into 10 zones and provide you with a sample step-by-step massage. Finally, you'll find out how to use massage to help you or someone you love through life's little and not-so-little challenges.

The ABCs of Massage

In This Chapter

◆ Keeping your approach warm and gentle

◆ Making sure your body is ready for a rubdown

◆ The do's and don'ts of massage

◆ The art of taking your time

It's time to clear the air about how difficult it is to give a good sensual massage …

It's easy!

Even if you said to us, "I'm all thumbs," you could still give your partner an incredible experience—the thumbs are great massage tools! All you need is the desire to give your partner pleasure and plenty of good old-fashioned patience. We'll take care of the rest.

In this chapter, we demonstrate a few essential tips and techniques so that you and your partner can begin to explore the path to pleasure. Just remember this: Always be caressing and gentle, and let your hands do the talking. We'll explore the material covered in this chapter in much more detail later in the book, but here you'll find enough information to get you started.

"A" Is for Approach

Your approach will create the mood you want for the sensual massage. Imagine two scenarios: In the first, you say sharply, "Hey! Do you want a massage? I've got 20 minutes, so hurry up." In the second, you gently ask, "Would you like me to make you feel relaxed and warm all over? Climb into the bed and close your eyes ..."

In the first situation, you've probably already made your partner tense, and that's the last thing you want to do when initiating a massage, particularly a sensual one. Instead your approach, or invitation, should already begin the process of relaxing your partner, as the second scenario demonstrates.

Finger Tip

Think of your partner as a cat: No cat owner in her right mind would grab her kitty, brush it with a wire brush, then expect it to stay on her lap purring with pleasure. Any cat worth his sardines would lash out with his razor claws, then run off and hide. Approach your partner in the same way you would approach a kitty: gently and sweetly.

How you approach your sensual massage partner depends upon your moods, his or her availability, and the setting. It's even possible that your partner may need some coaxing or cajoling to focus in on what he or she wants from a massage. Is he tired from swinging a golf club all afternoon? Is she anxious from studying for the bar exam all day? Is he moody from just getting the axe at work, or is she pouting because she's having a bad hair day again?

Once you've gently invited your partner to enjoy the touch of your hands, you need to make sure those hands are ready to touch your partner. Warm your hands—you can do this by rubbing them together or running them under hot tap water and then drying them. Likewise, any oils that you use should be warmed before you apply them. (We'll be discussing room ambiance in Chapter 10; we discussed massage surfaces and carrier oils in Chapter 4.)

Dr. Patti Says

You don't have to use words to invite your partner to partake of a sensual massage. Try some of these "pillow talk" ideas instead:

- ◆ Place a chocolate or invitation on his or her pillow.
- ◆ Lay lingerie on the bed while he or she's at work.
- ◆ Sling your favorite massage towels over the foot of the bed.
- ◆ Place a bottle of massage oil on the nightstand.

Take It All Off?

You will want to decide what level of undress feels comfortable for you both. How much or little you bare really depends on what kind of massage you're looking for. There's nothing wrong with wearing sweats or hiding behind/under huge towels or wearing workout gear such as skin-tight pedal pushers with a tummy-revealing top. Or if you're after a more sexy sensual massage, consider wearing a teddy (women) or silk boxers (men). Of course, another option is taking it all off—that's a perfectly acceptable thing to do!

You'll probably both want to settle on the same level of undress before you start the session. And don't forget that you can always take your clothes off, layer by layer, later.

Kevin tickles Martha Ellen with a rose as they demonstrate one level of undress.

(Robert Dunlap)

Dr. Patti Says
If you want to engage in massage for relaxation or healing, with no sexual undertones, then by all means wear clothes. If not, you might be sending mixed signals. If you want to use this sensual massage as time for foreplay, then wear sexy lingerie or bare it all. Of course, for some people clothing on the body is more appealing and alluring than nudity.

Trista and Gene, much in love, tease each other and show you yet another level of undress.

(Robert Dunlap)

"B" Is for Body Etiquette

When it comes to body etiquette, think clean. Here are some basic places on your body to inspect and upgrade if necessary:

Ouch! _____

Don't ignore those piggies. Craggy and uneven toenails can dig in if you use your feet or gag you if toe-sucking is on your agenda. You can drag your feet along your partner's skin and rip her to shreds if you haven't properly groomed. Imagine kissing a toe and finding a sharp object or even green cheese! Yuck.

- ◆ **Clean up your act.** Step one is getting clean. That may mean a quick shower or a long premassage bath. You may also want to review Chapter 18, where we guide you on the art of the sensual bath.

- ◆ **Nails.** Make sure that you trim your nails. File them so that they are smooth and then test them on your inner wrist to check for jagged edges or hangnails. If you have long nails and don't want to cut them, practice stroking your partner in a way that won't hurt him, or try a tickling motion or something that causes pleasure, such as a stroke using the back of the nail, instead of digging in with your talons. The simpler and shorter the better.

- **Whiskers.** Guys, listen up: You don't want to leave your sensual massage partner with razor burn instead of heart palpitations of love, do you? If you have a beard or mustache, make sure it's trimmed; otherwise, shave away that five o'clock shadow or two days' worth of stubble.

- **Basic oral hygiene.** Imagine that you've put on your black teddy and heels and are preparing to give your sexy partner the touch treatment of a lifetime. Just as you approach his head to stroke his cheeks and temples, he opens his mouth and breathes day-old pizza and beer breath into your face. Ugh! The moral of our little story is this: Brush your teeth, use a mouthwash or a tongue scraper if needed, and floss daily. If you haven't noticed that dentistry has moved out of medieval times, you need to book that appointment for a cleaning, too.

- **Hands.** Rough hands require TLC before you put finger to flesh. If you are a car mechanic or a rodeo master you may have to work to get smooth skin. Most people will just have to make some minor adjustments to have hands that feel good to the touch. Use hand creams on a regular basis, and if you really want to do this well, do a good hand soaking. Soaking in a solution of sea salts will let your skin shed those old crusty particles that make it rough or dry.

- **Elbows.** Use the same sea salt solution that you used with your hands to soften those crusty elbows. Or try a loofah mitt to scrub the nobs into submission.

Goddess Helen Says

Try this recipe for smooth hands:

The day before giving your sensual massage, soak your hands for 20 minutes in salt-water, using sea salts and warm water as your solution. You can add essential oils, such as lavender or tea tree, to the solution if you want to. Lavender is relaxing and the tea tree is a natural antibiotic—good for healing cuts and little tears on the skin surface. Rub your hands together with the sea salt, which causes friction and helps to remove dead skin on both the inside and outside skin, letting the oils absorb. (You can also do this to your feet). Apply a hand moisturizer to replenish the natural oils that you have sloughed away.

After applying the moisturizer, wear a pair of cotton gloves to keep the gooey, wet stuff you've just applied on your hands rather than on the furniture, your clothes, or whatever else you touch.

If you like going to a salon for your beauty and skin treatments, ask for the paraffin hand dip, which feels weird at first (like, is this how aliens feel?) but then if you can surrender to it, it feels great. You'll look mahvelous, darling, too! You can also now buy home paraffin kits.

"C" Is for Commitment

You've got the relaxing music turned down low, the massage oil is warm in your hands, and you're ready to make your partner's head spin with pleasure. Now don't spoil the mood by thinking about the time. Set aside a few hours so that you can make the most of the experience. Although you shouldn't expect anything after your sensual massage other than the good vibes of having given or received pleasure, let's be candid: You never know what a great sensual massage can lead to ...

Choose whatever amount of time feels right. You'll be shocked at how quickly time passes when you are giving a sensual massage—especially for the person on the receiving end!

Here are some more tips to make your time together even better:

- Imagine as you are caressing your partner's body that you are actually massaging yourself. Would you want patient attentiveness given to your body?

Finger Tip

Set a quiet timer or use one of your CDs to let you know when time's up. Or invest in one of those gorgeous and soothing Zen clocks that let you record your own voice or that ring with a pleasant Tibetan chime.

- Listen to the sounds your partner makes, and distinguish from the oohs, ahs, and ouches. If you remain quiet you will learn more about your partner by giving a sensual massage then you could learn exchanging a thousand words. The touch of love says so much more than words could ever say, and if your partner starts purring, you know it's right.

- Always caress with long, slow, gentle strokes, and enjoy.

Sensual Massage Do's and Don'ts

Here are some other things to keep in mind to make the most of your sensual massage:

Do ...

- Ask your partner if he has any sore muscles before you begin.

- Find out if your partner has any ticklish areas, such as feet or midsection. If so, avoid a light touch in those areas.

- Be sensitive to your partner's response to the massage. If she starts drifting off to la-la land, let her go there.

◆ Relax before you dive into touch. Breathe a little, listen to some soothing tunes, or even sip some calming tea, such as valerian root or a chamomile.

◆ Be spontaneous if your honey wants to turn the massage into sex. You can pick up on the sensual touch part later.

◆ Be responsive to your partner's needs. If he isn't in the mood to give you a massage, be the giver this time. Same thing for if she's not ready to reciprocate—relax and give it a rest.

◆ Let your strokes flow into one another with no abrupt endings. Keeping both hands on the body at all times is your anchor for staying connected to your lucky massage recipient.

◆ Give equal time to each of the 10 body zones (see chapters 7 and 8 for more on these). The legs, arms, and shoulders should all get the same amount of your amazing touch.

Don't …

◆ Talk too much. If you do have to talk, speak softly.

◆ Jump right into a massage. You wouldn't jump into a pool of water without first testing the temperature, would you? Ask your partner if he or she is too cold or hot. Men are usually warmer than women are, but there are exceptions to the rule.

◆ Comment on how tight muscles might feel. If you come across a tight muscle, let your hands to do the talking. Work around the tight area, giving it a little more love and attention.

◆ Pour oil directly onto the body. This can be a bit of a shock, and it isn't as comforting as your hands gently gliding onto your partner's body with warm oil.

◆ Eat a heavy meal before receiving a massage. This can cause mild to severe discomfort while lying on your stomach. Instead eat a light meal a few hours before the massage.

> **Goddess Helen Says**
>
> My massage clients sometimes complain that other massage therapists tell them, during a massage, that their muscles are tight or say something such as, "Oh my God! How can you walk around with such tight shoulders?" This sort of comment will only succeed in creating tension between you and your partner. If you want your sensual massage to be a pleasurable experience, focus on the positive. Negative talk only interferes with relaxation.

Slow Down, You Move Too Fast!

It takes mental training, the right attitude, and a commitment to share a sensual massage. The key? Slowing it all down. If you were to take just one piece of advice from this book, it should be this: Take your time. Stop the frenzy.

Try the following suggestions for slowing down:

- **Breathe.** To avoid pain, to endure the pressures of a certain massage technique or placement on the body, to clear the tensions of the day, or to get into the mood for lovemaking, breathing is a key element. Breathing helps you to focus on pleasurable sensations, keeps the attention on body, and promotes good circulation.

Finger Tip

Move more slowly and we guarantee your life's going to improve. So is your sensual life.

- **Use music as audio wallpaper.** Use music to set the mood, keep the pace, enhance the romance, and soothe jangled nerves. You can select music for pepping up the energy or easing into a slower pace for this special time together.

- **Light and darkness.** Too much light in a massage area can be distracting. In Chapter 10, we discuss selecting and preparing the right locations and settings for your sensual massage. Having the proper lighting will help you get in the mood for massage.

- **Time management.** Oh boy. We know how challenging it can be to take the time out for play. Managing time is one of the greatest challenges of today's insanely busy world. Whew. No wonder your back is aching for a massage of any kind.

Dr. Patti Says

A lot of people are overwhelmed by the idea of slowing down—in or out of the bedroom. They believe that if they slow down they'll have to give something up, with life-altering results. If you're one of those people, then consider reading *The Power of Now*, by Eckhart Tolle, who has magically captured the essence of being in the moment, of staying in the present, and living in the now. When you focus on the present moment, there is no fear, worry, or panic. There is only the experience of what is. That same state of being present, of centering in the moment, is what sensual massage can be. Slowing down into the presence of "now" can take you to new heights of awareness, allow you to exchange with a partner at a level that you may never have reached before, and permits an intimacy that can provoke deep, lasting joy.

Let yourself indulge in time for sensual massage and make it count. You'll reap more than just rewards, we promise.

The Least You Need to Know

- ◆ Your approach to sensual massage will determine its outcome.
- ◆ Get squeaky clean before you lay your body down on the massage table.
- ◆ Set aside enough time so that you can both enjoy the experience.
- ◆ Slowing down is a key to successful sensual massage.

Chapter 6

Different Strokes for Different Folks

In This Chapter

- ◆ The incredible human hand's design for touch
- ◆ Using other body parts as massage tools
- ◆ How to reduce strain and avoid pain
- ◆ Mastering the four basic strokes
- ◆ Determining your intensity, style, and type of touch

Did you ever think that the craggy nubby thing called your elbow would turn into a cute massage tool? Knees, elbows, chins, forearms—even foreheads— no part of your body is going to seem the same after you read this chapter!

There's more to a massage than most people think. In addition to mastering the stroke itself, you need to know how much pressure to apply and what kind of rhythm to use. And if you don't position your and your partner's bodies properly during the massage, neither one of you will be relaxed or comfortable.

Are you ready for the inside scoop on what it *really* takes to give a good massage?

Need a Hand?

Open your hands and take a close look at them. If the inside of your hand is facing you, the heel of your hand is the bottom fleshy part that meets the wrist and thumb. The area below the fingers is known as the mound of the hand, and it's just like the ball of your tootsie. Both the heel and the mound are essential massage tools. The side of your hand can also be instrumental for certain massage strokes, as can the flat surface in the center of your hand under your mound, which is known as the palm.

If we didn't know better, we'd say that the human hand was designed for giving sensual massage!

(Hrana Janto)

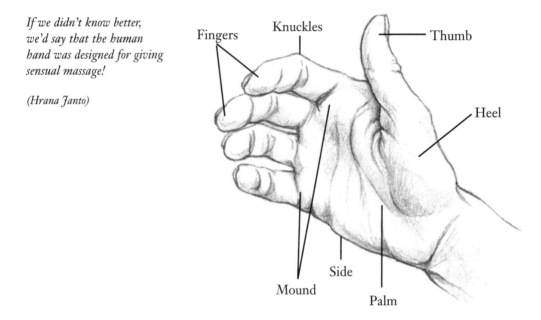

If we didn't know better, we'd say that hands were created specifically for giving sensual massages. Even if you just rely on your knuckles—both the ones at the bottom of the fingers and in the fingers themselves—you can propel your lucky massage partner into bliss. Knuckling is a good way to relieve pressure and create oh-so pleasant sensations.

Equally essential to massage are the fingers—they're handy helpers that are perfect when you want to target smaller areas or do more delicate work. You can use all of your fingers together like a gripping device for squeezing and kneading, or you can use the fingertips for a stroke that's similar to finger painting. Your fingers can really push deeply into the flesh to release tension, relax the muscles, or even just prod and tickle.

And don't forget your fabulous thumb—it's a little tool all its own for getting into those tricky areas between the shoulder blades, the neck, and supplementing the work that your fingers do.

Don't Forget About Your Feet, Elbows, and Chin

Although hands really are the perfect massage tools, other body parts can be used to create wonderful sensations and to give your hands a break when they get tired. For instance, anything you can do with your hands and fingers, you can also do with those feet of yours. Your heels can push and prod your partner's derriere, or you can sit behind him and push your tootsies into his aching, tired shoulders. *Ahhhh*. You as the giver will feel the delight of stretching out your gams while your fortunate partner will be ooohing and ahhing as he lets go of all that tension carried in the tops of the shoulders.

If your legs are strong, you can use your knees to create powerful sensations quite effortlessly. Making sure you're not putting your full weight on his body, press your knees into your partner's buttocks. Move those knees gently up the sides of his rear end. (If you get really good at this, you may be an applicant for a new job at the Shiatsu center near you.) It's a nice way to say "I love you" without words.

> **Ouch!**
>
> Never, never put pressure on a bone, especially the spinal column. And even if your weights are evenly matched, be cautious about using the full weight of your body on your partner. In particular, avoid putting a lot of pressure or weight on the areas above the waist on the back and front of the body, where the organs such as the kidneys are situated.

Other Ideas?

Another wild idea is to lay your entire body across his back, and rub a dub dub! You'll discover other ways to create wonderful, sensual sensations once you begin to explore—we promise!

Less Strain, More Gain

Positioning, or how and where you place your body while giving a massage, is probably one of the most important things we can show you how to do. The more you can do to minimize your strain, the more pleasure you and your partner will feel. Believe it or not, if you just use your hands or fingers, you're going to run out of steam pretty quickly, left to wonder what the heck you did wrong or to despise the act of sensual massage. That's the last thing we want to happen. Instead we want you to feel great and make it last a long time.

There are a variety of positions you can get into while giving a massage. You may find it easier, depending on each situation, to stand, sit, kneel, straddle, or lie next to your partner. Each position has its limitations. If you are straddling your partner's body, for example, you can reach only certain areas of his body. If you are kneeling near his lower back, you'll probably have to scoot down to reach his lower legs and move up to reach his shoulders, and you'll only be able to reach one side of his flanks, ribs, or legs.

When standing, keep your back straight and whenever necessary bend your knees rather than your back. Keep your feet apart for a firm base.

(Hrana Janto)

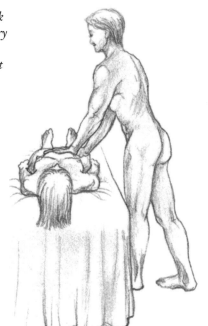

When sitting keep your back straight, and don't hunch over.

(Hrana Janto)

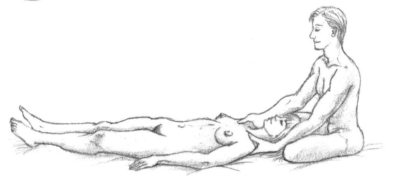

When straddling your partner, keep your back straight, and avoid scrunching or curving your spine. You'll probably want to alternate this position with other positions. Don't collapse on your partner while straddling across him or her.

(Hrana Janto)

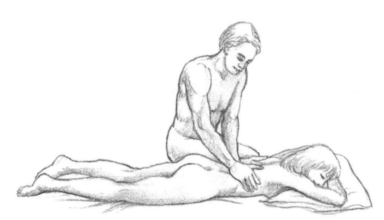

Use a pillow under your knees and behind your calves for support and comfort when kneeling. Keep your spine straight, body upright, and move your whole body with your massage strokes.

(Hrana Janto)

You are limited to where you can reach when lying down. This is perhaps the most intimate position of all, letting your body touch his, like spoons, or facing your partner's body.

(Hrana Janto)

You will have to move yourself around to access the full body of your partner. Standing beside or at the ends of your partner, especially if you use a professional massage table, will help you to reach with longer strokes. Experiment with the different alignments, and you will eventually discover your favorite way to give sensual touch. You may even decide to use them all, integrating the many ways to share touch and intimacy on different occasions.

Finger Tip

The best way to avoid tiring yourself out or putting too much strain on your hands, fingers, legs, or any other part of your body is to vary what you do. You may want to push the flesh with your fingertips for a while, then switch to knuckling, or kneel into it or use your forearm. Think about all of the possible ways that you can stimulate a response in your partner, and figure in all of your own body parts that you can use. You can try kneeling on your partner's buttocks, or thumbing behind his shoulder blades, tickling the back of his neck with those talons, kneading him in the front of his thighs, dragging your palms over his chest, even using your lips as tools to create shuddering sensations all over his skin.

All the Right Angles

It's important to follow these principles for angling yourself as the giver of the sensual massage. It's not just about using your hands. Hands and fingers are the extensions of other movements and abilities:

Goddess Helen Says

There are times when a light touch is called for, such as to show the more playful parts of your sensuality. Other situations command a deeper probe, whether it's to create relaxation, help in the release of built-up tension in the muscles, or to change the mood of the massage. And, by the way, changing intensity from one stroke to another may also help you focus better.

♦ **Use your whole body, not just your hands.** When you conduct a massage, your whole body moves from its center.

♦ **Use your hips to help you move.** If you are reaching across the body, let your hips sway to take you there. Maintain a straight spine as much as you can, elongating your back as much as possible.

♦ **Support those knees.** Using a rolled up towel or small pillow on the backside of your knees when you are in kneeling mode will keep your feet from falling asleep. Staying comfortable will allow you to focus on your partner and not on your aches and pains.

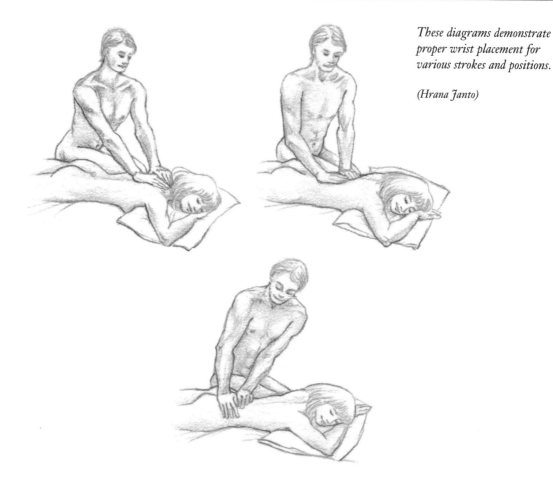

These diagrams demonstrate proper wrist placement for various strokes and positions.

(Hrana Janto)

◆ **Make sure that your wrists are placed just above and in the same angle as your hand for proper touch.** Lean into the angle of your hand with your body weight placed above the hands. If you follow the motions and movements of your hands with your whole body, you will avoid strain and keep in good alignment. Bottom line: Don't rest all of your weight on your hands, but do lean into your hands to let your weight flow with their every move.

◆ **Make sure that your shoulders are relaxed.** Good shoulder posture is a must, otherwise you're the one who's going to need the massage!

◆ **Keep your hands loose and relaxed.** Use all the many parts of your hands, switching from the teeny little pads at the tips of your fingers to the palms, mounds, sides, and thumbs. Or use a tennis ball to release built-up tension and muscle tiredness. Hands do tire, so give them a rest now and then.

If your hands ever get tired while you're giving a massage, then you're not using proper body alignment. Relying on your hands alone is a surefire route to disaster. Rely more on your body weight to create pressure, rather than pushing with your fingers or thumbs.

Let's face it, if you're a 90-pound woman trying to give a pleasant massage to a 300-pound lout of a partner, you're not going to get too far with your hands alone. And if heavy Harry is massaging you, he'd better position himself carefully to find the proper leverage to avoid crushing your bones.

Stroke It!

Now that you know how to position yourself to get the most of your body, it's time to learn some basic strokes. We recommend four basic strokes that you can easily learn without going to massage school. We'll refer to these same four strokes—and variations on them—throughout the rest of this book.

Touch Term

Rhythm means how fast or slowly you rub, stroke, push, or knead.

In addition to describing the strokes, we'll also suggest what kind of *rhythm* to strive for when using them. However, you shouldn't be afraid to try your own rhythms out as well.

Roll It

Let's start with the first stroke—we call it roll it. This is a long, gliding stroke that soothes the muscles and relaxes the body while also increasing circulation. You can use it on most parts of the body, but it is particularly effective on the back, chest, arms, and legs.

To perform this stroke, push using the whole hand—from the heels of your hands through to your fingers—and on the return pull back through the fingers to the heel of the hands. Repeat. You can perform this stroke up and down the length of the body or across it.

Try to keep your rhythm slow and languid when rolling it—these strokes feel better the slower you go. You don't want to rush. Don't just do one or two strokes and then stop; instead, repeat the stroke 15 or so times to get your partner purring. Conjure up a slow waltz in your mind to set the rhythm of this one—slow, easy, and gliding.

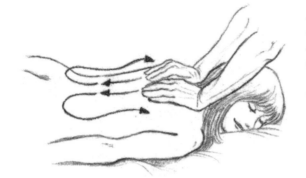

Roll it's long, smooth strokes are sure to make your partner sigh as she/he starts to unwind.

(Hrana Janto)

A variation of roll it uses the same movement, but instead of a long stroke, it's horizontal—like finger painting, but we promise that it's more fun when you're "finger painting" the back of your partner. This stroke is great for nagging neck and back muscles. For variety, try speeding your stroke up a bit, making it peppy.

Use your fingers to make small, circular, rubbing motions along the sides of the spine and between the shoulder blades. If you don't get a sigh here from your partner, we'd be surprised.

Knead It

The second stroke is knead it, and it's a classic Swedish massage maneuver (see Chapter 1 for more on Swedish massage). This stroke feels great on the shoulders, thighs, and buttocks, where you can easily lift and gently squeeze the muscles.

To perform the knead it stroke, lift and squeeze the muscle between your thumbs and fingers using a single hand or alternating between both hands. You can use your knuckles to push into the flesh where the muscle is tighter.

Knead it involves lifting and squeezing the muscles between your fingers and thumb.

(Hrana Janto)

Move your hands in a figure-8 pattern while kneading the flesh. Try to keep a moderate tempo—faster than the languid movements of roll it but not so fast that your movements are jerky.

Goddess Helen Says

We discuss oils, powders, and lotions you can use for your sensual massage in Chapter 4, but if you don't have any on hand, grab some massage oil from your local health food store. Steady, though—use just enough oil to fit in the cup of your hand. It's easier to add more if you feel the skin drinking up the oil than to mop it up if you use too much.

Tap It

Tap it is just like it sounds—tapping and beating on the skin using light to medium pressure. The stroke, which is also known as tapotement in the Swedish massage system, works wonders on the back, shoulders, and feet. Use your fingers for a lighter tap and your soft fist for a firmer tap or beat. It can also be used on chest, legs, and buttocks.

Start lightly and increase pressure with feedback from your partner. Use the fingers for a lighter tap and a soft fist for a firmer tap or beat. Beat like a drum—you choose the tempo.

You can vary the pressure of the tap it stroke and even use your fists or knuckles instead of your fingers.

(Hrana Janto)

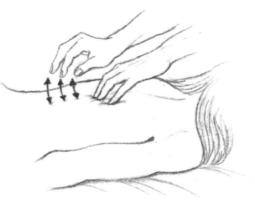

Brush It

Brush it is a whisper of a stroke, like using a feather. Slowly trail your fingers, using alternate hands, up your partner's back, legs, chest, and arms. You can use the brush it stroke up and down the length of the body or across it.

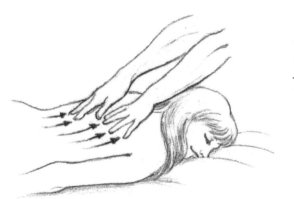

Brush it involves long, slow strokes up and down or across the body, using your fingers, hands, or any other body part.

(Hrana Janto)

If you really feel like getting playful, use your hair to simulate the brush it stroke on your partner's body.

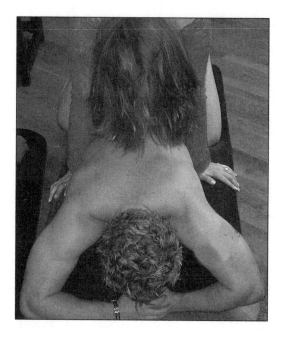

Hair dragging is a surefire lure into ecstasy.

(Robert Dunlap)

Finger Tip

Be generous with your touch when massaging your partner and listen to her responses. If she is moaning with pleasure, that's probably a sign that she wants you to continue with that stroke. Always remember to stay with slow, rhythmic strokes—not fast and jerky ones that can interrupt the flow. Be creative and gentle.

Play Around

For now, play around with these strokes until you're comfortable with them. In Chapters 7 and 8 we'll run through some complete massages—step by step—including how to position yourself to get the most out of your movements.

Now just because we have walked you through some basic strokes and suggested where to use them, you should feel free to develop your own style as you go. If you only want to do a part of the body in one sitting, fine. If you want to go faster or use strokes on body parts that we don't recommend, you may discover a whole new way of tempting touch on your own. As long as you don't push too hard on sore places, put pressure on the bony regions, or crash on your partner with a 10-ton force, you can play with this all you want.

Your Personal Pleasure and Pressure Points

Now that you know *how* to touch your partner, let's take a minute or two to consider *where* to touch her. In other words, you'll want to figure out where on your partner's body touch feels pleasurable, where it's ticklish, where it hurts, and where it's a turn on.

Different areas of the body feel touch differently. Here are some standard sensations that people have when touched on various parts of their bodies:

- ◆ **Tickle points.** Tickling is fine, when that's what you want—a gentle tickle can relax or arouse. But the deep poking kind of tickling should typically be avoided during a massage. Common tickle points are the bottom of the feet, under the arms (underarm), and the ribs.

- ◆ **Relaxation points.** These are the areas on the body that when touched induce a sigh of relief from the receiver, even a sound of *ahhhh*. They make you feel good. They let you let go. They open up your ability to release tension, which is probably why everyone wants to be touched on those points. Think about how good it feels to have your shoulders or elbows touched, for instance. In addition to the shoulders and elbow, common relaxation points are the back of the neck, scalp, back, hands, and feet.

> **Dr. Patti Says**
>
> The television sitcom *Ally McBeal* had a running joke about the backs of the knees as the secret to arousal. Ally wasn't far off! Touching neglected areas such as the back of the knee can help you to relax. Those parts of yourself that are designed for "work" (like the hands and heels of the feet) become zones for sensuous pleasure when they are lightly stroked or tickled.

◆ **Erogenous or pleasure points.** Okay, you're probably wondering, "Aren't they zones?" Nope. They are points, or specific places on your body that, when triggered, can arouse you. Touching an areola or nipple can send a woman (or a man) into ripples of sensations that can stimulate the desire for sexual contact. Erogenous points can include the abdomen, side of the neck, earlobes, lips, breasts/nipples, inner thighs, and the genitals.

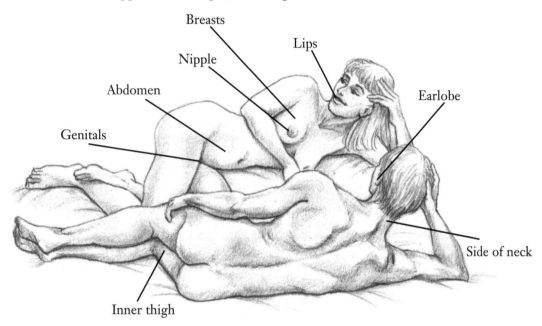

Touching any of these pleasure points can make your partner swoon.

(Hrana Janto)

◆ **Pressure points.** In most Eastern medicine systems, there are designated points and pathways (often called meridians) that carry energy to and from the organs. If you've ever had acupuncture, reflexology, or an acupressure massage, you've had your points pushed. Many people believe that massaging these points can heal the body.

Show and Tell

Because you want to achieve the desired mood during your massage, it's important that you and your partner are aware of what parts of your bodies evoke different sensations. Talk to your partner about where those four types of points—tickle, relaxation, erogenous, and pressure—are on your bodies. Or use the following diagram to point them out to your partner or indicate them with a pen or pencil. You can even use different colored ink to indicate the different types of areas, such as pink for tickle points, blue for relaxation points, red for erogenous spots, and green for pressure points.

Use this diagram for playing show and tell with your partner. Point out your tickle, relaxation, erogenous/pleasure, and pressure points.

(Hrana Janto)

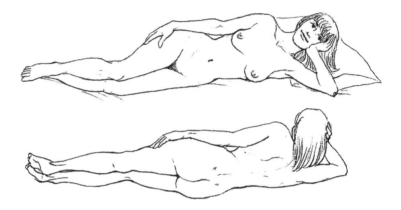

Goddess Helen Says

Do you want to see tension melt away from your partner's shoulders? Here's a technique you can use. Have him lie facedown, and then rest your hands on his shoulders. Sink your thumbs into the shoulders directly under the earlobes. If his muscles are tight, this might hurt, so ease into it and tell your partner to breathe deeply as you push. Move your hands to the side about an inch and repeat, continuing to the entire process about four times. This technique releases in that famous tension-holding muscle called the trapezius. From there you can move down the side of the spine, hitting points about 1 inch on either side of the spine.

Handle With Care

If you touch a point on your partner's body where she says it hurts, proceed carefully. Although some pain does feel good, it's also a signal that something's not right. So if you do hit a pain point and your partner tells you it's too much, ease up. If she's enjoying a little ouch, then go for it. It's important to find your own balance, as the last thing you want is to cause pain or harm during a massage.

You'll also want to avoid applying too much, if any, pressure on other parts of the body. No-no's may include the following:

Spine

Ribs

Anklebones

Eyes

Kidneys (just above the waistline on the back)

Stomach and abdomen

Carotid artery (just to the side of the neck)

Breastbone (that part between the breasts in both men and women)

Diaphragm

Clavicle (collar bone)

Wrists

Elbows

We've mentioned this before and it's worth repeating: Avoid leaning on your partner to support your weight. Imagine your sweetie placing 220 pounds of body weight on that delicate floating rib—talk about ouch! If you are on the receiving end and your partner is applying too much pressure or is using you as an armchair, tell him to stop. Sensual massage is meant to be for pleasure.

Find Your Flair

When it comes to sensual massage styles, you are going to evolve your own. Styles for sensual touching can be as different as hairstyles. The best way to discover how well your hands work on your partner's body is to practice. Don't be afraid to try out all of the methods, approaches, and techniques we mention in this book until you find the one or more that suits you.

Once you find your primary touch style, indulge yourself in it. Really jump in. Don't judge what you do or how you are doing it. As long as you stay focused on what your hands are doing and your connection with your partner, you'll be fine.

You may discover, for instance, that you feel more confident or even do a better job when pushing deeply into the tissues, making you more of a deep tissue massage-giver. Or you may like the long slow strokes of the Swedish method. You may even develop a combination of strokes, rhythms, and intensities or special movements on your partner that can change with time or that will become a style that is uniquely yours. For example, you may like to make little butterfly wings with your fingers on her flesh or pull on your lover's earlobes, or even use your mouth more than your fingers. Go for it!

The Least You Need to Know

- ◆ The hand makes a wonderful massage tool, as do your other body parts.

- ◆ Proper positioning and alignment reduce body strain.

- ◆ The four basic strokes are roll it, knead it, tap it, and brush it.

- ◆ Avoid all forms of harmful and painful touch.

- ◆ You can develop your own unique style for sensual touch.

Chapter 7

Facedown, Back Up: Massage Round #1

In This Chapter

- ◆ Final pre-massage checklist
- ◆ The five zones of the body facedown
- ◆ Massaging the five zones

In this and the next chapter, we suggest a sample massage routine. Even though we provide steps for you to follow, you should know by now that we strongly encourage you to go with the flow and do whatever seems right at the moment. Don't be afraid to try different strokes—even using parts of the body besides your hands. This step-by-step massage should be your starting point—to give you an idea of the basics—so have fun with it!

We begin the massage routine with the receiver's body lying face down. In Chapter 8, we flip the body over and stroke the face-up side.

Note: Although we use the female pronoun throughout this chapter for ease of reference, either gender can be the first to receive the massage. For the sake of fairness, we'll shift to the male pronoun in Chapter 8.

Your Pre-Massage Checklist

Like a pilot preparing for take-off, you'll want to make sure that you and your "passenger" are prepared for your journey. Here's a pre-massage checklist for you to run through.

❏ **Comfort:** Begin by making sure your partner is comfortable. Does she have enough pillows for support, such as under her feet, or a face cradle to keep her head supported?

❏ **Temperature:** Is she warm enough? Make sure the temperature is set to her comfort level. If you get too hot or cold, you know that you can easily strip down or add layers of clothing to warm yourself up.

❏ **Alignment:** Make sure that she is lying facedown in a straight line.

❏ **Trouble spots:** Ask your partner if she has any injuries or sore places on her body. Avoid touching the injured areas and spend more time massaging the sore parts.

❏ **Grounding:** Prepare yourself both physically and emotionally. In Chapter 14, we'll discuss setting your intention, including how your thoughts and feelings can get transmitted through your hands. Now is the time to sit quietly and to take some deep breaths while you set your intentions for your sensual massage experience.

Finger Tip

In the massage routine that we walk you through here, the giver is in the kneeling position. If you prefer to sit beside your partner, that's okay. You may even feel like changing from one position to another. That's up to you, your setting, and how your body feels. Find the position (or positions) that feels the most comfortable for you and go with it.

❏ **Warm hands:** Before you touch a molecule of her skin, rub your hands together to warm them up. No one wants icy fingers and hands on their flesh.

❏ **Lube up:** Have your oil ready to apply. Put a dab of oil about the size of a quarter on your own palm. Rub your hands together. Remember never pour oil directly onto your partner's skin.

❏ **Protect your knees:** Remember to get a soft pillow to put between your feet and your bottom if you plan to kneel during the massage (which is our recommended position throughout this sample massage). It really helps!

❏ **Get slow:** Slow down. Sensual massage, unlike some other forms of touch, is all about taking your time. Whether you intend to get down and get sexy or you just plan to make your sweetie relax, it's all about going slowly.

❏ **Keep in flow:** Consistent contact with your partner's body is important. Keep one hand on your partner at all times, even when reaching for more oil.

The Five Zones

We are starting facedown, back up to give you a leg up on the receiver's comfort. It's easier for the receiver to relax into the massage this way. If you are giving the massage, testing your skills on the back is going to help you prepare for the more vulnerable and softer parts when you flip your partner over.

We've divided the body into ten different zones—five facedown and five faceup—to make it easy for you to get around it. Remember, spend time on each of the zones, providing pleasure to your partner and giving equal time to every part. However you are going to find some delicious places where you may want to spend longer, and that's okay with us.

Zone One: Legs and Calves

Begin by kneeling at your partner's feet, facing her soles. Don't forget to use a pillow under your buttocks for your comfort. Decide which leg to work on first; once you finish the massage steps on the first leg, you'll switch to the next leg and repeat these steps.

Finger Tip _____

Forget about the feet! We'll cover them in Chapter 8. If you like, as a nice way to say hello, greet the feet with your hands, warming them up.

Calves

Legs do a lot of work and can really get tired and sore. The calves, in particular, love a good rubdown. However, the calves can be very tender when touched with pressure, so go easy.

Ouch! _____

Always avoid putting pressure on the back of the knee. Do not massage over varicose veins. Avoid anything that appears swollen or is sore to the touch. Hairy legs require gobs of lube, so be sure to use extra oil on the hair before you glide along her sore calf muscles.

1. Use the roll it stroke up and down the entire leg 10 to 15 times, leaning forward and into the stroke to warm up the leg and increase circulation. Once the leg is warm and you feel comfortable doing the stroke, limit the stroke to the calf—from the ankle up to the back of the knee—at least a couple of times.

Calf roll it.

(Robert Dunlap)

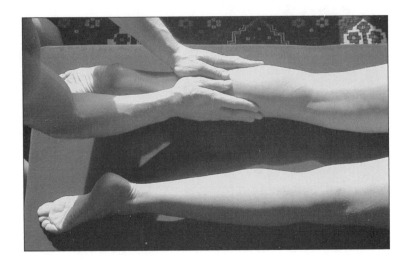

2. Move to the side of the leg that you are massaging and begin performing the knead it stroke up the calf. Now might be a good time to quietly check in with your partner to see whether she would like you to apply more or less pressure.

Calf knead it.

(Robert Dunlap)

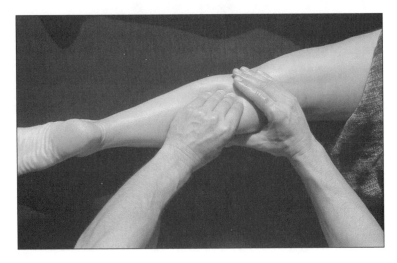

Upper Leg/Back of Thigh

The upper leg is the home of the hamstring—the thick, strong, and usually very tight muscle that is sensitive to touch. If you sit long hours, this can become very contracted, causing tightness and attracting injury. The back of your upper leg is also an erogenous zone, including that sexy inner thigh. Oooh, keep breathing now.

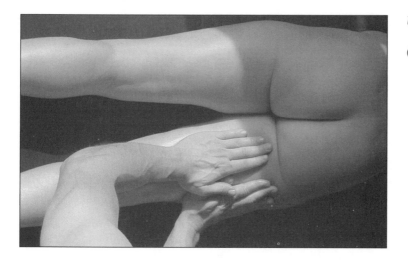

Upper leg roll it.

(Robert Dunlap)

3. Still kneeling to the side of the leg, start with the roll it stroke up and down the upper leg. Do this 10 to 15 times.

4. Next use knead it, again up and down the length of the leg. Try following a figure-8 pattern as you go. Repeat once or twice.

5. Switch back to roll it, this time focusing on the inner thigh. Reaching across her leg, pull the inner thigh toward you. Remember to reach and pull with your entire body, not just your hands. Move as high up the inner thigh as you feel comfortable.

6. Finish the upper leg with brush it for your finale.

Now switch sides and repeat steps 1 through 6 on the other leg. Be sure to keep in body contact with your partner when you are moving around her body.

Finger Tip

Using brush it lightly up the leg starting from the ankle and going to the top may arouse your partner, so be prepared!

Goddess Helen Says

If you are in the middle of giving your sensual massage and are working from the bottom up, facedown, your partner's arms may begin to lose sensation. When her hands are resting above her head, on the floor, or on any other platform, they will eventually go numb. If the arms are down by her side, she has a better chance of maintaining circulation in the arms. Give her a pillow so that she doesn't have to use her arms to support her head.

Zone Two: Buttocks

The gluteus maximus, a.k.a. butt, is one of the thickest muscles of the body, if not the thickest. Usually this is tight, especially if you are athletic. Sitting for hours at a computer or behind the wheel doesn't help either, as it results in poor circulation.

To begin massaging the buttocks, kneel at the side of her body, on the same side as the cheek you're about to touch, with your knees facing her body perpendicular to it. To change cheeks, change sides.

1. Use a light roll it stroke to spread the oil around, or repeat the whole leg roll it from the ankle to the fleshy mounds. Do this 3 to 10 times.

2. Start at the top of the fleshy part of the buttocks and use the knead it stroke, alternating between using your fingers and your knuckles.

Move to the other side and repeat steps 1 and 2 on the other cheek.

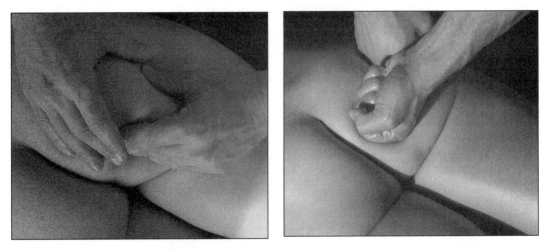

Knead it on the buttocks, using knuckles for deeper sensation.

(Robert Dunlap)

Dr. Patti Says

A good playful spanking may add fire to your touch, if your partner likes that kind of thing. Spanking brings blood flow to the muscles; it's not merely the practice of sado-masochists. If you and your partner are open to exploring what I like to call "S&M lite," go for it. Get out the old ping-pong paddle for a bout of fun, use kitchen gadgets that provoke different sensations, or invest in some serious gear. The buttocks are the perfect place to explore S&M lite.

Zone Three: Back

The back is your basic platform for all other body parts—those thick, dense muscles support the whole body, making this a perfect place to do your deep plunge into touch. If you can learn to do all of the backstrokes, you can become a master of the whole body.

Although you shouldn't massage the spine itself, the muscles next to the spinal column (about one inch from the center line) produce some of the most intense sensations in the whole body when touched. The shoulders also love to be touched, as they carry a huge amount of tension and stress.

Kneel at the top of your partner's head so that you're looking down at her from her head to her toes. Your hands should be pretty warmed up by now; however, if they're not, rub them until they feel warm to you.

Position yourself at the top of your partner's head.

(Robert Dunlap)

1. Start with roll it, 3 to 10 times, with a nice long gliding movement from the shoulders down to the waist. Then spread your hands around the hips, pulling back along the sides of her body, and finishing up at the shoulders. You may want to keep gliding in one unbroken movement, ending up around the shoulders. Try not to break contact while you massage the back. (This may be a good time to tell her to remember to breathe, in case she's headed for outer space by now.)

Use roll it down the whole back and then back up again. Caress your partner's buttocks as you change direction.

(Robert Dunlap)

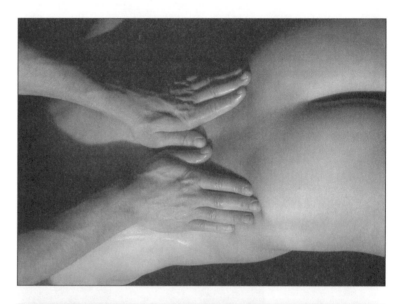

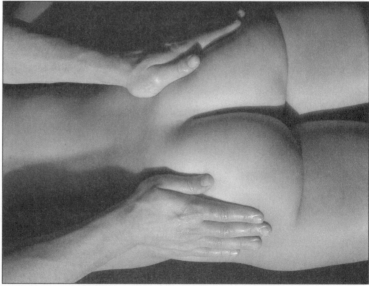

2. Next, you can scoot to the side of her body and use the roll it stroke from the side. This will give you access to her ribs, stroking across her body from one side to the other. Try some finger painting here as well.

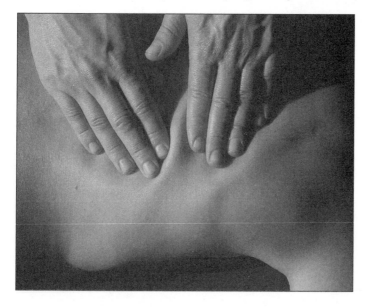

Finger painting, a variation of roll it, feels great on the muscles next to the spine.

(Robert Dunlap)

3. Now use knead it on her sides, reaching across and working on the opposite side, just like with your roll it stroke. Knead along the sides up into the shoulders, coming back around the other side of her body, while maintaining contact.

4. Try out some tap it along the fleshy part of the back and over those tight shoulders. Be sure to avoid tapping on the kidneys, which are located just above the waist.

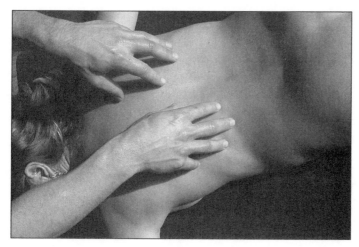

Use tap it anywhere on the back except above the kidneys.

(Robert Dunlap)

5. Repeat steps 2 through 4 on the other side of the back.

6. Return to the top of her head and finish up with some energetic brush it, using your fingers or nails if you have them. You may want to do brush it from the lower back up to the shoulders and neck area for your finale.

Use brush it on the back for another pleasure delight.

(Robert Dunlap)

Zone Four: Neck

The neck supports the head, each day holding up about 10 to 15 pounds of weight. (And you thought your brain was just mush.) If you spend long hours in front of a computer and have poor back posture, your neck is going to absorb the strain. Poor sleeping positions, such as lying on your stomach with your head to the side, also contribute to neck strain.

> **Ouch!**
>
> To avoid neck strain, encourage your partner to move her head from side-to-side from time to time. If her neck gets sore, she may need a softer surface to support her head, or roll up a towel and let her use it for head support under her forehead, elevating the whole head.

The neck can be an erogenous zone, especially when touched lightly with a feather, a well-oiled finger, a warm breath, or your lips.

To begin working on the neck, remain kneeling in front of your partner's head; or if you prefer, you can also sit to the side of her neck for better angles in your reach. Again, use a pillow to support your body if you are kneeling.

1. Start with knead it. Place your fingers on the sides of the neck, starting at the base and moving up to the back of the skull. You might want

to knead in small circles using your fingers or your knuckles. Don't hesitate to move from the neck to the upper shoulders.

2. Use brush it down the back of the neck (we don't recommend tap it on the neck).

Use knead it on the neck to open things up.

(Robert Dunlap)

Zone Five: Head

Like the neck, the bony head can be a high-tension area. Also like the neck, the head is one of the more sensuous parts of the body.

Remain kneeling at the top of your partner's head.

1. Move the scalp—not the hair—with your fingers in a circular motion based on the knead it stroke.

Make circular motions using your fingertips to create awesome pleasure on the head.

(Robert Dunlap)

2. Play with the hair, letting it sift and roll through the fingers. Pretend to wash her hair, using a scrubbing motion. Go as long as you like, but be sure to do at least a full minute. Releasing tension in the scalp goes a long way to complete relaxation.

3. If you have long hair, you can drag it along your partner's back, shoulders, and buttocks for a real sensation party.

Goddess Helen Says

At the back of the head you will notice a little rim, known as the occipital ridge—you can feel where you fingers actually sink in. Putting your hands there is comforting and relieves tension. Ask your partner for feedback when you very gently push on it. No nails, now. Go easy and hold your pressure on the points for 30 seconds to a full minute.

If your partner is in facedown mode it's going to be difficult to reach the full scalp. Hang on until it's time to do the pancake flip and get it then.

The Least You Need to Know

- Before your begin your massage, run through our pre-massage checklist.

- How you approach the five facedown zones is a key to your success as the giver.

- Each of the five facedown zones has unique characteristics that must be considered before you touch them.

Chapter 8

Back Down, Faceup: Massage Round #2

In This Chapter

- ◆ The five zones of the body faceup
- ◆ Massaging the five zones
- ◆ Wrapping up or switching roles

Once you've finished massaging the first five zones, it's time to turn your partner over and start all over again from the other side. Softly whisper something like, "Honey, it's time to turn you over now." He may be asleep, so be careful not to startle him.

Once you have turned him over and have gently positioned the legs and arms, align his body in a straight line. Gently pull his neck to straighten it, making sure the chin is dropped forward to lengthen the neck. If your partner has long hair, be sure to move those locks out of the way from under his back. Put a pillow or rolled up towel under his knees for support. This will help to keep his body in alignment for your touch.

Just as with the front side of the body, you should focus on your partner's comfort. Check in to make sure he's warm enough but not too warm. Keep those oils at a nice warm temperature. Check how much time you have left on the CD and change it if necessary. Also make sure that you are comfortable, using that pillow under your knees. If you feel the urge, go to the bathroom now (and have your partner do the same if he needs to), before you begin round two.

The Five Zones, Backside Down

This side of the body is more vulnerable to injury—things are softer, more easily squished, and even more delicate, like the shins, the breasts, the genitals, and the clavicle. Try to avoid putting too much pressure on those more sensitive parts. Your massage mate's going to love it if you spend equal time on every delicious zone on this side of the body.

Zone Six: Feet and Legs

Few things in life feel better than a good old-fashioned foot massage. Throw in some tender strokes to the legs and upper thighs, and maybe even some toe-sucking (called "shrimping" by those in the know), and you've got yourself a recipe for some real sensuality!

Feet

Feet are bony, tender, and ticklish. Because we shove them into shoes all day, they tend to be tight and tender and suffer from a lack of circulation. Nonetheless, feet are notorious for being highly sensitive as an erogenous zone and are prone to tickling sensations, especially in between the little piggies.

To begin your faceup massage, kneel at the bottom of the feet, facing the soles.

1. Begin by rotating the ankle joint by moving the foot from side to side, first one way and then the other. Do this a few times.

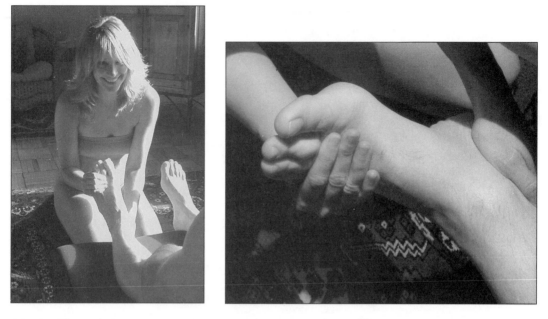

Martha Ellen is about to rotate Kevin's ankle. Notice how she holds his heel as she turns the foot.

(Robert Dunlap)

2. Grasp the top of the foot, near the toes, and use roll it to open up the soles of the feet. You can either use your fingers or your knuckles; using the knuckles allows you to apply more pressure, which should be firm but not too deep, especially if your partner is ticklish on his feet. Do this 10 to 15 times.

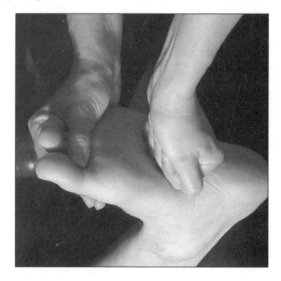

Performing roll it using your knuckles allows you to apply more pressure.

(Robert Dunlap)

3. Switch to the knead it stroke, moving from the arch of the foot to the toes. Move slowly, like a little snail inching up the shaft of a plant.

4. Moving on to the toes, gently rotate each one, first one way, then the other.

Gently turn each toe to loosen them up.

(Robert Dunlap)

Finger Tip

While stroking the feet, you may want to place your partner's on your knees (if you are in the kneeling position). This gives you better leverage to touch his foot, and he can relax his leg.

5. Then use roll it to rub up and down each toe a few times.

6. Knead the toes as you did with the soles.

7. Finish off the toes and foot with the brush it stroke on the top and underside of the foot.

Repeat steps 1 through 7 on the other foot.

Goddess Helen Says

Special foot massage balms or oils can enhance your massage. If you use a peppermint, eucalyptus, or wintergreen scented foot oil, be sure that you wash your hands thoroughly before touching the face or the eyes. Similarly, wash your hands before engaging in sex if you use one of these oils.

Legs

A lot of tension gets stored in the upper leg, which has some of the body's longest muscles. And, of course, the inner thigh is a highly erogenous zone.

To begin massaging the legs, kneel to the side of the leg you wish to touch first. To give you more leverage so that you can push more deeply, elevate yourself from your kneeling position, leaning up and over his legs. When you are working on the thighs, remove the pillow under his knees to gain better access.

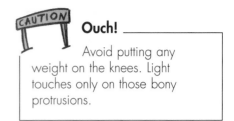

Ouch! _____

Avoid putting any weight on the knees. Light touches only on those bony protrusions.

8. Start with roll it, stroking up and down the entire leg several times. Make sure you get to touch all the way up to the hips, the outer and the inner thigh, and down to the ankle. Don't miss any of the leg—it's going to feel really good.

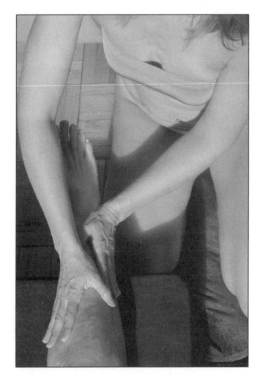

Use long slow strokes up and down the entire length of the leg.

(Robert Dunlap)

9. Focusing on the lower leg, do a few rounds of knead it. Work from the ankle all the way up to just below the knee.

10. From your same position, knead the thigh. Try following a figure-8 pattern over the entire thigh—both the inner and outer portions. If your partner's muscles are particularly tight, you can use a variation on the knead it stroke with your knuckles.

Grasp and knead with your fingers and thumbs on either side of the shin bone.

(Robert Dunlap)

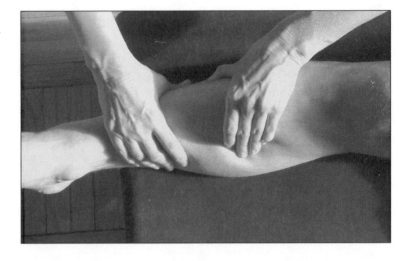

Knead both the outer and inner thighs.

(Robert Dunlap)

Use your knuckles to push more deeply into the thigh muscles.

(Robert Dunlap)

11. Next use roll it on the inner thigh. Use long, slow strokes beginning at the inside of the knee. This is one of the most sensual strokes on the body—really lean into it and try to create a gliding sensation. If you have time or are in the mood, you can also put some frosting on the cake and do some brush it strokes for a while.

Switch legs and repeat steps 8 through 11.

Zone Seven: Stomach

This soft tissue area contains a lot of organs, so go lightly here. Rubbing the stomach can alleviate constipation and ease symptoms of PMS. This part of your body can be erogenous, especially on the lower abdomen.

Start on the right side of your partner's body, kneeling to the right side of the ribs.

1. Start out with roll it, stroking in a clockwise direction beginning at the navel, circling out, going up to the diaphragm, and ending at the hips. Do this around 10 times, very slowly and applying light pressure. This will release the digestive tract by going in the same, clockwise direction, helping to unblock gas, congestion, or constipation.

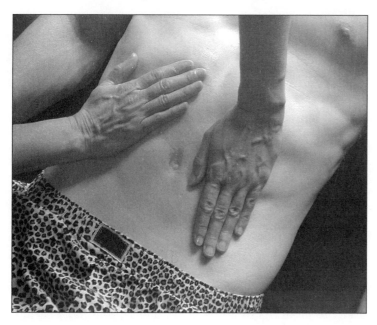

Move your hands in circles around that tummy zone.

(Robert Dunlap)

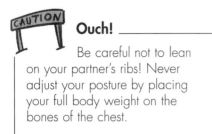

Ouch! _____

Be careful not to lean on your partner's ribs! Never adjust your posture by placing your full body weight on the bones of the chest.

When using roll it across the body, you can reach down and massage the lower back, too.

(Robert Dunlap)

2. Next lift yourself up and lean over the top of his body so that you can gently knead the opposite flank or ribs.

3. Then do roll it across his body, reaching underneath his ribs, and delicately scooping the flesh with your hands like sifting sand for shells. For added pleasure, you can even do roll it on the lower back when you do your scooping.

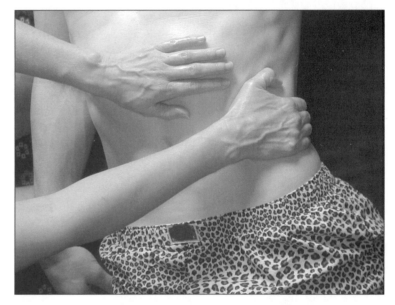

Repeat steps 1 through 3 from the left side of his body.

If your partner's lower back hurts, this can be a good time to draw his knees up and put his feet flat on the massage surface for a few moments. It's a great way to create some relief on the back of the spine.

Zone Eight: Chest

The chest can be very sensitive to pressure, so take it easy here.

Begin by kneeling at the top of his head.

1. Start with roll it from the shoulders to the stomach, pulling your hands around the sides of the ribs, and back up to the top. You can add a rocking motion while you pull back up. Repeat 10 to 15 times.

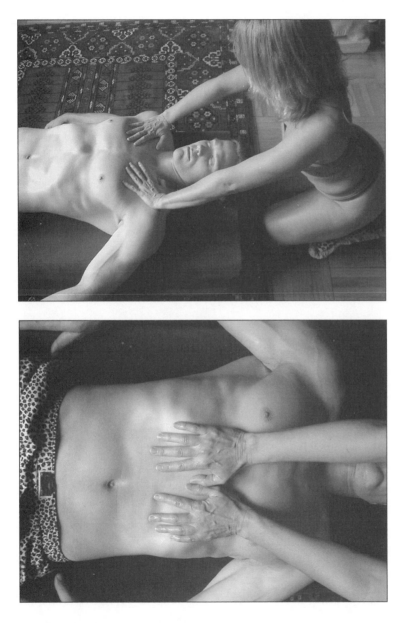

Starting with the shoulders, roll it down the chest and back up again.

(Robert Dunlap)

2. Touch around the breasts in circular motions, opening the web of your own hands and letting the natural contours of the breast tissue fall around your hands. Avoid touching the nipples, unless you don't mind arousing your partner. (In therapeutic massage, the nipples and areolas—the colored parts that encircle the nipples—of the breasts are a no-no.)

3. Next, do some tap it on the chest, which can feel both awakening and relaxing. You can also do a little teasing here—as you are moving down his chest, lean into his face.

CAUTION   **Ouch!** _____

If your guy has a hairy chest or stomach, make sure that you oil the hair—that's right, the hair not the skin. Also watch out for the breastbone here, especially if you are doing any tapping on the chest. The clavicle, or collarbone, is a delicate one, which doesn't usually respond positively to pounding or pressure of any kind. Go easy if you massage it.

Zone Nine: Arms and Hands

Feel free to massage the arms and hands before you massage the chest. The order doesn't matter.

Arms

If your massage mate beefs up those biceps and triceps at the gym, a relaxing arm massage will have them sighing with pleasure. Even if your partner doesn't work out, arm massages can be surprisingly delightful.

Make sure that your partner's arms are at his sides, and kneel on the side of his body.

1. Start with a nice long roll it stroke, from the wrist all the way up to the neck. Repeat the stroke several times.

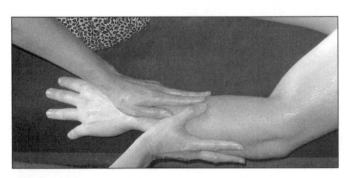

Roll it from the wrist all the way up to the shoulders.

(Robert Dunlap)

2. Follow up with knead it, up and down the arm, once or twice.

3. Now focus on the shoulders. With one hand grasping his wrist, hold up his arm; with your other arm knead his shoulders.

4. Finish off the arms with another round of roll it, throwing in a brush down the entire length.

Hands

Your hands tell a story about who you are and what you do, whether you're a brain surgeon, engine mechanic, painter, or sculptor. Like the hand, the palm is a secret map of who you are.

Remain at your partner's side to massage his hands:

5. Grasp both sides of your partner's hand with both of your hands and gently pull down it, massaging the palm with your fingers.

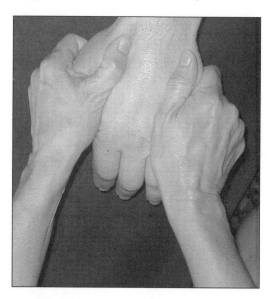

Stroke your partner's hand with both of yours.

(Robert Dunlap)

6. Next, turn the palm faceup (not too forcefully) and hook your fingers in between his fingers to open up the palm. This should feel very relaxing to your partner's hand. Use the knead it stroke on his palm with your thumb while your fingers remain interlocked. Before you leave this position, rotate the wrist a few times.

Interlace your fingers with your partner's and gently rotate his wrist.

(Robert Dunlap)

7. Now turn the hand over and knead the top of the hand.

8. Finally, just as with the toes, rotate each finger one at a time. Then gently use roll it on each finger, pulling the finger toward you.

Use pulling strokes on each finger to open them up and release tension.

(Robert Dunlap)

Switch to the arm and hand on the other side and repeat steps 1 through 8.

Zone Ten: Neck, Face, and Head

When you get to the neck, face, and head, you'll probably want to change oils, using those that we recommend for the face (see Chapter 4), or stop using oils altogether. If your partner has long hair, be extra careful to move it out of harm's way.

Kneel at the top of your partner's head. You can also sit straddling the head, with your legs spread down by his shoulders, which adds sensual option for body contact. For some people, letting your partner's head rest in your crotch area can be very erotic and suggestive.

Finger Tip _____

Germaine Morgan, a Malibu hairstylist, gives this tip: A scalp massage is one of the most sensual things you can do. "It can turn a man into butter," she says. And guess what else? Her female clients complain that their hubbies never talk. She says, "These men never stop talking when they're in my chair." She's on to something—maybe wives can give scalp rubs to locate those latent male communication centers!

1. Begin at the top of the shoulders and knead the shoulders in a circular motion, working from the shoulder to the back of the neck.

2. Gently cradle the back of your partner's head and turn it to the side. Use a variation of the knead it stroke with your fist, stroking down the side of the neck to the shoulder while the head rests in your other hand. Turn the head in the other direction and repeat.

3. Bring the head to the center and knead the back of the neck up to the occipital ridge.

4. Start massaging the temples—the area to the side of the eyes—with a gentle stroke, making circular motions the size of a small coin. Go in one direction, then reverse it.

 Ouch! _____

Make sure that your partner doesn't mind you using oil on his or her hair. If he or she does, tie it up in a barrette, a bandana, or a small towel. You can even place a towel on top of the head and touch the towel rather than the hair.

Be gentle as you stroke the temples in circular motions.

(Robert Dunlap)

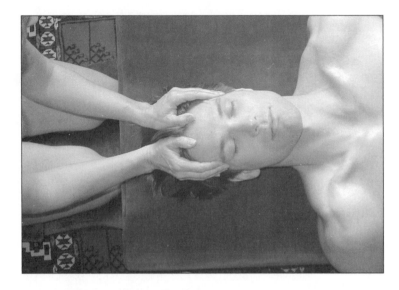

5. Continue the circular strokes on the cheeks, forehead, and jaw.

Apply circular strokes to the rest of the face, including the cheeks, forehead, and jaw.

(Robert Dunlap)

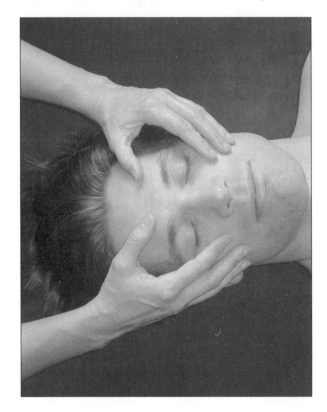

6. Brush the chin, cheeks, jaw, and forehead to relax him further.

7. If you want, you can now repeat the scalp massage from Chapter 7, focusing on areas that you couldn't reach when your partner was facedown. Otherwise, skip to step 8.

8. Finish up with a little massaging on the ears, rubbing the earlobe between your thumb and the index finger. Remember this is a very sensitive body part, and one that can affect your health and healing.

Ouch!

Take special care with the eyes. Never push on the eyes. And never let oil get near the opening to the eyes—even a little bit of oil can cause serious problems.

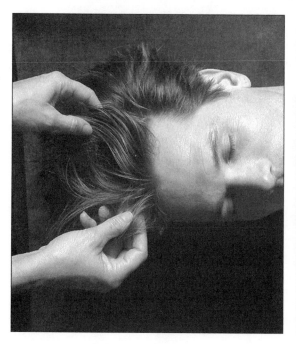

Pull gently on the hair to stimulate the scalp.

(Robert Dunlap)

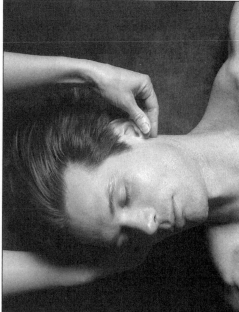

Don't forget to stroke those earlobes.

(Robert Dunlap)

Mix It Up

Once you have taken the time to try out the many different ways and places to do roll it, knead it, tap it, and brush it, you may want to get a little more fancy with your touch style. We've already described some of them, without naming them, in the preceding steps:

◆ Roll it can also become a stroke called "Sun and Moon," which uses alternating full hand circles in a clockwise direction. We described this stroke on the stomach.

◆ Knead it can morph into stripping, a stroke which uses the thumb and index finger to inch like a snail up a part of the body, such as the calf.

◆ Use a soft fist instead of your fingers to do tap it.

◆ Use your forearms or elbows instead of your hands, which allows you to apply more pressure. Minimize oil with your forearm and elbow to avoid slipping. If your partner wants even more pressure, cut out the oil altogether so that you don't slide.

You can integrate all of these strokes once you gain mastery over the basics.

Invent strokes of your own and do your own digital creating. The sky's the limit, really, on how clever you can get using the four basic strokes and taking them to a new dimension. Even just the speed of touch, the pressure you use, and the pattern and direction of your hands can make a big difference.

You and your sensual partner may even want to make up special names for your touching styles. Use names of dance steps, for example, like a quick fox trot using a syncopated movement, a slow waltz to go slowly with a glide, or a mambo. Such shared language will heighten the experience.

Wrap It Up

If you agreed that you were both going to give each other a massage, it's now time to switch roles. Before doing so, however, it's probably a good idea to take a brief break, so you each have a chance to re-ground yourself and prepare for the next stage.

If you are feeling particularly romantic by now, plant a soft kiss on your partner's mouth and see what happens from there …

The Least You Need to Know

◆ Take a break before moving on to the other side of the body.

◆ Each faceup zone has its own special characteristics.

◆ Use special oils or avoid using them altogether when massaging the face.

◆ After giving a sensual massage, you may need a break before you switch roles and begin again.

Chapter 9

Special Sensual Situations

In This Chapter

- ◆ Finding relief during pregnancy and after childbirth
- ◆ The art of baby massage
- ◆ Recovering from physical illness
- ◆ Quelling the symptoms of menopause
- ◆ Aging and the need for touch
- ◆ Giving yourself a massage

You already know that massage makes you feel great, and humans have known about the healing powers of touch for thousands of years. It makes sense, then, that massage can be used to get us through difficult physical or emotional times. This chapter will highlight some of the real benefits from a sensual massage during those more trying times in your life. Whether it's the birth of a new child, becoming menopausal, or recovering from illness, you can use sensual massage to help you cope with and even conquer what ails you.

Your partner can be your best ally if you are suffering from any of the conditions we are about to discuss. Or you can be the caregiver, using the knowledge gained in this book to help those around you feel better.

Having Our Baby

Pregnancy is physically and emotionally straining for a pregnant woman. Not only is she carrying around the weight of her developing fetus, she's also gaining weight on other parts of her body, and probably feeling drained. Being pregnant is not a sickness, however, it takes a lot of energy to sustain a woman during the nine months of gestation. With all of the hormonal shifting and body changes, it can be a stressful ride for Mom-to-be. She needs nurturing fingers on her flesh.

We've already told you that sensual massage can relieve tension, stress, fatigue, and pain—all of which pregnant women usually experience. Many women who are pregnant also suffer from lower back pain from the added weight they're carrying around. Plus, they experience breast swelling, which often provokes neck, shoulder, and upper backaches.

In addition, massage can help reduce morning sickness and can even help the growing fetus: Toxins get routed through the placenta to the developing fetus, but a good rub-a-dub-dubbing can help to drain the mother's lymphatic system and reduce the chances of birth defects caused by harmful toxins. Even self-massage is a helpful relief from the aches and strains of the pregnancy.

Follow your typical massage routine or the one described in Chapters 7 and 8. However, instead of lying facedown, have Mom-to-be lie on her side and support her belly with pillows.

So re-read Chapters 7 and 8 to choose what moves she feels will alleviate some of her distress. Ask her to tell you what she needs, where it hurts, and what feels good. This is no different from any other sensual massage. Mommy-to-be is going to love you for anything you can do to make her body feel more rested, comforted, less tense, and soothed.

> ### Dr. Patti Says
>
> Although sensual massage certainly can be a prelude to sexual touch, there are huge health and healing benefits to a nice rubbing. Use the information in this chapter to help out a friend or tune in to your mate during times of high stress or pain.

 **Ouch!** _____

> We do not recommend massaging the protruding region of a pregnant woman's stomach and uterus.

> ### Goddess Helen Says
>
> For specific strokes on a pregnant woman, use roll it down the spine, knead it on the shoulders and neck, roll it on the legs, and knead it on the thighs, hips, and buttocks. You can add a scalp massage with roll it on the temples, and for the feet and hands use roll it and knead it.

Any carrier oil is suitable for pregnancy, and so are rose, geranium, lavender, and chamomile essential oils. Use some or all of these in equal proportions, for a total of 30 drops in 2 tablespoons of carrier oil.

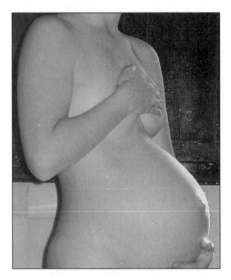

A pregnant woman can find sensual massage a soothing way to take a break from the strain.

(Robert Dunlap)

Post-Partum Rubdown

Sensual massage is also a perfect antidote for those post-partum woes, such as depression, general body pain and exhaustion from just having popped a kiddo out of the body, and those common demons of constipation and hemorrhoids. The bottom line is that she's going to feel more rested and experience less tension and better energy flow and circulation if you use sensual massage.

Be sensitive. *Don't* dig your fingers into those delicate or very sore body parts. Be careful, too, that if she had a C-section, her obstetrician has approved her receiving a massage.

Don't Forget the Baby!

The word is now out on massage on a baby—the crying and diapered kind, not your girlfriend "the babe." Recent research shows that babies who are massaged by their moms go into sync with their mothers' sleep patterns, thanks to the release of the hormone oxytocin. This natural wonder chemical helps to create bonding during breast-feeding and helps to propel the infant into this new sync-up with its mother. That's enough reason to rub your newborn while you're catching up on the morning news, isn't it?

Put your baby down on a soft surface, such as your bed or the crib. Begin massaging the baby's head and face, so that you can maintain eye contact. Make sure the room is warm enough and minimize noise distractions just as you'd like to have it if you were getting a rubdown.

If you decide to oil up your little one, use a carrier oil such as almond oil. Place your fingertips or thumbs on areas too small for your whole hand. Keep all of your strokes slow and smooth, and watch for baby's response to your touch. Baby will let you know if he likes it or not, by smiling, cooing, writhing, or jumping for joy.

Roll it in circles on the scalp, working over the whole head, go up and down the arms and legs, rotate those tiny fingers (softly and gently now), and take a gander at using the "Sun and Moon" stroke we described in Chapter 8 on that fat little belly. Using roll it up and down the back is always soothing and will make you feel really good, too, by inhaling that wonderful scent that's oh-so baby!

A little rub-a-dubbing on your infant (clothed or not) may even put him to sleep. Now there's something every parent needs!

When Chicken Soup Is Not Enough

Chicken soup may help you feel better if you're sick, but if that's not your style, think about the benefits of touch. If you or your massage partner have just undergone surgery or are ill and in recovery, touch is essential. Of course, whether your honey just ran a marathon, was in a car accident, just had her bunions removed, or has the flu, she has to be handled with plenty of TLC—emphasis on the *care*.

CAUTION

Ouch!

In recovery from recent surgery there are some recommended protocols we want to mention. Don't ever massage over sutures, wounds, or sites of intense pain. Although some experts may tell you that touching the sites of a wound, surgery, or any other invasion of the body is good for you, we advocate that you leave that up to the professionals.

How you touch someone who is sick or recovering is going to be determined by what happened to her or his body during that illness, injury, or surgical procedure. However, careful is your watchword no matter what state he or she's in.

As noted previously, sensual touch can help to improve circulation, oxygenate the blood, and remove those dratted toxins that cause disease later on. Some people even claim that it can reduce swelling and help to break down scar tissue. We don't think that doing a gentle session of touch on your sweetie will erase any stretch marks, but the key here is to boost circulation and energy flow around the body. If you're sick or recovering from surgery, even just the knowledge that someone cares enough to take the time to touch you will help you feel better and get better faster.

Honey I Can't Sleep

If you are one of the millions of people who suffer from lack of sleep, or even if you're just dreaming of that trip to Paris but are trembling with fear about the horrors of jet lag, you're in luck. As noted in Chapter 3, massage stimulates the release of hormones that help you catch your Zzzzs.

Sleep is an important part of the healing process, so using a tender touch on your partner's body after surgery or a long illness will not only feel good but, by helping him or her sleep, will further contribute to his or her recovery.

Dr. Patti Says

The memory of being touched in an unpleasant, unwanted, or violent way can remain in your body years after the actual experience. For example, many people who suffered from sexual abuse as children store traumatic memories in their thighs. When other people touch their thighs, memories of the traumatic experience may surface. If you or your partner experience strong negative feelings when certain parts of your body are touched (and we're not talking ticklish underarms here), then you should consider seeking professional help. Your counselor may recommend professional radical body therapy such as Rolfing, which literally moves tissues and releases huge emotional blocks.

The Change or the Curse?

If you are a woman and over age 50, you've probably already reached menopause. If you're in your early 40s the biological clock is probably still ticking, but the batteries are running low, meaning that you're in that period called *peri-menopause*. For you, hot flashes are *not* nights of unabashed passion, and days of stable moods are a fleeting memory.

Many women who are peri-menopausal suffer from just as many of the symptoms of body wracking as those with pre-menstrual syndrome (PMS). Those symptoms include tension, aching in the groin and lower back, headaches, depression, mood swings, bloating, and breast tenderness. You name it, it's probably something you can blame on either PMS or

Touch Term

Peri-menopause—the months or years leading up to the actual onset of menopause, which is technically one year after your last menstrual period.

Dr. Patti Says

Did you know that one of the best ways to alleviate some of the negative symptoms of both PMS and peri-menopause is an orgasm? Well, that's what the sex doctor is ordering!

peri-menopause, wrong or right. And despite all the best intentions of medicine to help you out during these phases (yes, there are hundreds of drugs and over-the-counter remedies now), one of the best ways to feel better is a little sensual massage.

Combating stress, fatigue, aching muscles, tired bones, a worn out nervous system, and lack of anything remotely like a desire to be sexual, sensual massage is a good way to find some relief.

Up Against the Clock

If 80 million Americans have their way, no one will age in the twenty-first century. However, even with the billions of dollars spent on anti-aging products and cosmetic improvements, you can't win this battle in the end. And although you can gracefully age, as many do today, with supplements, exercise, or spa retreats for lifelong rejuvenation, you are going to reach a point where the skin sags and that flesh that used to point straight forward as an arousal cue now points South on your compass. As people age, they might feel tender more often, tire more easily, and walk with a slower step. (If you do keep a healthy lifestyle with exercise, diet, and a positive mental attitude, things will not deteriorate as quickly as they could.) When you get older, you can really benefit from touch.

Finger Tip

Some progressive hospitals have started using massage as part of their treatment programs for Alzheimer patients. One study showed that massaging the neck and shoulder areas reduced symptoms such as pacing, irritability, and restlessness.

Dr. Patti Says

Sexologists will tell you that just because you age doesn't mean that sex stops. To the contrary, the "use it or lose it" phrase applies here. One way to boost the engines for both sex and keeping those feel good hormones alive is ... of course, you figured it out, didn't you? It's sensual massage.

Seniors often don't think they have the right to touch or be touched. They may have lost their spouses or they might live in contained environments where, except for those enlightened few, the idea of an intimate union is all but forbidden.

Seniors need skin-to-skin touch as much as supple-skinned youth. Seniors often have chronic aches and pains, can be creaky and cranky, and go slowly. If you are massaging Granny or Great-Uncle Louie you will want to go easy, slow down, and be gentle with those sore, tight places. Here are some tips for how to give massage to an elderly person, and how to maximize their comfort while they receive touch pleasure.

♦ You will need to add extra padding to the massage surface, such as a double comforter under the sheet or a foam pad under the bedding.

♦ You can always massage Gramps in a chair, having him sit facing the back and lean on it.

♦ A scalp massage or a rubbing all over the head will bring great relief.

♦ If your older friend is frail, his circulation may be poor. Use roll it up and down the back and especially on the limbs to get that blood flowing. Pay attention to the feet and hands, too.

♦ Older people may be shy about being touched. It's not necessary to remove clothing, and focusing on the hands, head, and feet may be a lovely way to create comfort, both psychological and physical.

♦ We recommend using the roll it and knead it strokes for maximum pleasure on your older massage mate, especially on the back and shoulders where everyone seems to hold tension, no matter how old.

♦ If you use oils, carrier oils such as evening primrose or sesame are best for older skin types. Sesame also is good for rheumatism and arthritis. Be sure to dilute either of these oils (at around 10 percent) with a lighter carrier oil such as grapeseed.

♦ Sensual massage may be the perfect foreplay for an older couple looking for a gentle way to get their boat launched for a night of lasting pleasure.

Seniors can also help others and at the same time help themselves: Older folks who hold babies and touch them not only help the babies but also get from the experience a sense of purpose and worth. Integrating sensual massage will increase your quality of life no matter how old you are!

The Art of Do-It-Yourself

If you don't have a regular partner or if getting touched by another human being gives you the willies, then self-massage may be your best bet. Touching yourself may seem like an odd idea, especially with all this talk about back-rubs. But let's face it. Your body needs sensual soothing touch as much as anyone's does. Without a trusted massage buddy around, doing the solo thing can be a wonderful way to relax, feel more alive, promote self-healing, and ease those achy muscles.

For some, solo sensual massage is the entry ramp onto the highway of self-sexual pleasure: the "M" word—masturbation. Masturbation, or solo sex, is not only its own sexual outlet as a normal healthy form of sexual expression, but it also is the foundation for all shared sex with a partner. This may be the very foreplay you've been longing for on those cold, winter nights alone by the television set, hoping for oh-so-much more.

Sensual self-massage might sound difficult—so how do you reach around and ooze into those tight shoulders?—but it's not really that hard. For a sufficient sensual self-massage, allow plenty of time. Be sure to give yourself at least 15 minutes to nurture your whole body, front and back, bottom to top, with oils and toys, if you wish.

Follow the pattern we used for partner massage in Chapters 7 and 8 as much as possible, starting from the feet to the head then flip yourself over. Or use these easier-to-do-on-yourself guidelines:

- ◆ Lie faceup on your back, and focus on your head, scalp, face, and chest first. Use your favorite oils, just as with a partner, to create the mood you want. Of course we are assuming that you've gussied up the place and done all the necessary steps to have an uninterrupted time at it, such as dimmed the lights, turned off all machines, set the temp control, and locked up the kids or pets.

- ◆ While lying faceup, continue to rub and caress yourself along the front of your torso, on the belly and abdomen. Don't forget to massage your arms and hands. Spend a good amount of time on those paws, both the palms and tops, to soothe your tension.

Finger Tip

A tennis ball can be a self-massager's best friend. Lie on the ball (or balls) wherever you feel tension, strain, or stress. We guarantee that you'll feel more relaxed, calm, nurtured, and soothed after rolling around on a tennis ball for a while.

- ◆ Now sit up and pay some attention to your legs, starting at the feet and toes, working your way up. Spend a lot of time on the feet. They are probably your most overworked body part.

- ◆ Stand up and stretch your arms around yourself. Touch and caress what you can of your back. Draw oils or lotions around your ribs and smoosh some on your lower back where you can reach. If you bend down you can massage your buttocks and the backs of the legs. (Right about now you'll be wishing you had practiced your stretches in yoga class a little more.)

◆ If you want to get fancy, buy some massage toys. Some of our favorites are rollers, claws, knuckles, or heavy duty devices that you can plug into the wall socket for powering up your reach. Hitachi wands or Panabrators do the trick just fine.

The Least You Need to Know

◆ Aches and pains associated with pregnancy can be alleviated using massage.

◆ A gentle massage can help you recover from illness and surgery.

◆ Menopausal symptoms may be benefit from sensual touch.

◆ As you age, don't stop touching.

◆ With a little practice, sensual self-massage can feel great.

Part 3

Sensual Stagings

So far we've focused almost exclusively on the body's sense of *touch*. But to really make the most of your sensual massage, you need to attend to the other senses, too: taste, smell, sight, and hearing. That will involve selecting the right location for your massage, choosing the appropriate lighting, popping some mood music into the sound system, and pulling some tasty treats out of the pantry. Preparing for your foray into sensual pleasure may take a little effort, but we promise you that it's worth it.

Chapter 10

Location, Location, Location

In This Chapter

- ◆ Finding suitable places for your massage
- ◆ Getting your space ready
- ◆ Making all the necessary preparations
- ◆ Gathering the right materials
- ◆ Following certain principles to make it a success

When it comes to preparing a space for your sensual massage, the possibilities truly are endless. We can say this with confidence because we've been coaching couples for decades on how to bring the elements of sensual touch into their relationships. Whether you choose a French provincial boudoir or the workout room in the basement really doesn't matter. What does matter is how you prepare the room or space, what tools and accessories you bring to the process, and how carefully you plan. This chapter is going to get you started on finding and setting up locations for sensual massage that are going to help you move into the mood. It doesn't have to be the Taj Mahal to feel luxurious enough for a grand afternoon or evening of sensual touch.

Pick a Place

Where you do your sensual massage may be just as important as what you do! Yes, that's one of the secrets to a successful journey into the pleasure and fun of touching someone else.

Don't get stuck in the rut of thinking that everything has to happen in the same place. Forget about your bed, if that's a place to crash and burn after party night, a hideaway after too many hours at the office, or an instant demand for sex. Instead, get creative. Sensual massage is going to require that you find places or settings where you can lie down and get naked or close to it, so the front porch is probably out of the question. However, creating the best location may be as easy as moving some furniture.

In picking a place, the eyes don't always have it. You'll need to use all of your senses when choosing the best location. Yes, you want to make sure the space is appealing to the eyes, but you also want to make sure that it's an appropriate temperature, and that there aren't any distracting noises or smells.

Goddess Helen Says

One woman, a lovely older client we'll call Marie, told me how her husband had set up a massage room in their house that was next to a noisy street. Just as they were getting into the relaxation of their sensual massage, booming music from a car idling outside rattled their teeth and the windows. They slammed the windows shut and laughed at how impossible it seemed at that moment to feel sensuous.

To create the best massage location, you need to not just consider the comfort of the room, but other factors such as temperature, outside disturbances, and the overall energy and ambiance the room creates.

Inside the Home

If you live in a private home in a natural location, a secluded deck might be the perfect choice. And if that deck overlooks a grand vista, all the better! Most of us, however, will have to find a serene location inside our homes or apartments.

Consider the following possibilities inside your home:

> On the (sturdy, please) dining room table
>
> On a massage table
>
> On the floor in front of the living room window

On the couch

On the kitchen counter

The ideal temperature for a sensual massage is 72°F. Set your thermostat/air conditioner to approximate this and you'll hit the optimal comfort zone for your body. Remember, too, that the person giving the massage will heat up faster than the person receiving, so use the recipient as your guide for when to adjust the temperature.

Consider the following additional factors when choosing a room:

◆ **Is the room quiet and private?** Are you constantly being distracted by noises from the outside world or noises from ticking clocks and other appliances?

◆ **Is the room big enough for your partner to lay down and you to comfortably move around?** You may have to move some furniture out of the way, especially that annoying coffee table that you're always stubbing your big toe on. When it comes to massage areas, size does matter.

◆ **Is the room clean and free of odors that would conflict with the aroma created by any candles and incense you plan to use?** Make sure the room is tidy and well ventilated.

◆ **Are there any are pictures or posters that interfere with the sanctuary you are creating?** If you would rather not remove them, cover them with a tapestry or veil.

Finger Tip

If it's quiet outside and the weather is nice, try opening a window to ventilate the room. If not, then a fan or air conditioner set on the "quiet" or "silent" mode can help, as long as it doesn't create a draft.

Goddess Helen Says

Remember that when you are giving a sensual massage you will be warmer than the person receiving the massage. The temperature of the room needs to keep both of you comfortable. In the summer, keep a fan nearby, and in the winter have a heater close by with extra blankets. Test the room with your wet finger in the air and adjust the temperature accordingly. And, of course, you can always make adjustments to the temperature and airflow as the massage progresses.

Outside the Home

You may want to get adventurous and take your sensual fun beyond your four walls. Bringing variety into any relationship stimulates excitement of all kinds. Plan ahead so you have plenty of towels, or a blanket to lie on, oils in airtight containers, and even a handy boombox with relaxing CDs to create the right mood. Throw your massage toys in a bag and pile in some mats or soft cushions if you like. We believe that the more creative you can get for where you do your sensual massage, the better.

Outside the home, you may choose to experiment with sensual massage in any of the following locations:

- At the beach on a blanket
- On an outdoor picnic table
- In the back of your truck, van, or SUV
- In the backyard under the moonlight
- On a weekend getaway at a lakeside cottage
- At the Ritz Carlton hotel
- In a cheap hotel in Las Vegas for an escape weekend
- On a camping trip in an RV or tent
- At a friend's borrowed apartment

> **CAUTION**
>
> **Ouch!**
>
> Although you may be brimming with enthusiasm about exploring a sensual massage out in the open, be wary of unknown settings. Some of the critters in the good old out-of-doors can be harmful or dangerous. Plants such as poison ivy, oak, or sumac can ruin even the loveliest foray into nature. Being prepared means knowing the dangers or safety of the space you select.

Dr. Patti Says

Bruce, a former client, relied on the art of sensual massage as a prelude for sex with his sweetheart, Annie. Every time she appeared at her Don Juan's, Bruce would have a surprise waiting for her in the kitchen—and I don't mean biscuits. Bruce preferred to do sensual massage in his kitchen, never in the bedroom. He insisted that Annie take off her clothes when she arrived at his apartment and lie down on the black marble counter, which he had carefully spread with thick, luscious towels and a soft cottony wrap.

Weird? Not really, when you realize that both Bruce and Annie loved the shared sensuality of their greeting each time they met at his place. Bruce's insistence on his kitchen for their reconnection was to Annie sweeter than the honey in the jasmine tea she drank after each massage.

We guarantee that once you get started doing sensual massage as a regular part of your routine, you're going to invent places for massage that right now you couldn't imagine. You may find that there is one special place, such as a part of your bedroom or dining area, that you like to use for sensual massage more than others. That can become your permanent massage nook.

Put Your House in Order

Once you've settled on a place for your sensual massage, you might need to take some time to straighten it up—in other words, clear up your clutter. You don't want clutter to block the flow of energy or dampen your aesthetics. Nothing kills the sensual moment like having to tend to a bleeding knee after you've tripped over a pair of smelly sneakers.

Regina Leeds, author of *The Zen of Organizing* (Alpha Books, 2002) writes that clutter is the enemy of peace and can help or hinder your success in life. That's pretty powerful stuff. When you create order in your home or office, you begin to experience peace, flow, and harmony in all aspects of your life. Easy? Not. Simple? It is if you take the time to learn how to make it happen.

Finger Tip

Get a good book on how to de-clutter your home— *The Zen of Organizing* is one of our favorites—and then set aside a weekend for the task. Once you do it, make sure to keep it up, as that can be the biggest challenge. We know you can do it!

Try these four simple steps to eliminate clutter in the primary room where you want to do your sensual massage:

1. **Take out the trash.** Gather up all of the stuff that you don't need and remove it from your space. You may have to take a deep breath, get out those huge green trash bags, and start hauling.

2. **Get things clean.** Preparing your space for a sensual massage is part of the process of feeling good about it. Hire a house cleaner if you don't have time. Or set aside a couple of extra hours on your next day off to dust, vacuum, scrub the chandelier, polish the mirror, do the laundry, or whatever needs to be cleaned off and up.

3. **Go shopping for accessories to do the job.** Get yourself some organizing containers for your stuff. If you arrange things into bins, or cute plastic boxes, wooden crates, or even metal trays, your place is going to get more organized.

4. **Arrange things nicely.** Find a balance in what you need to have in the room and take out what isn't necessary. Let "less is more" be your guide. Minimize the things you have around you and you are going to feel more alive, peaceful, and beautified in and by your space.

Now, take a look around you and smile. You did it.

Touch Term

Feng Shui is the Asian art of placement of things in a space to create balance and harmony. This ancient form for "healing spaces" has become very popular recently and there are many books and courses teaching its principles.

One great way to create order in your home or office is to use the principles and practices of *Feng Shui*. For example, just having certain colors placed around your living room can brighten it up and attract the right energy to that part of the room. Feng Shui will help you to remove obstacles or objects that block the flow of *chi*, or energy, throughout your space. And if it's way over your head to even conceive of doing this type of thing on your own, then consider hiring a Feng Shui practitioner. It's not only an excellent way to ring your chimes, it's sure to change the space you live in for the better. It can improve your whole life.

Chinese Menu Checklist of Massage Options

Once you've have had a chance to scout out locations, it's time to do a Chinese Menu Checklist for your massage. We want you to choose among the three types of approaches that you can use at home. They are our idea for how you can go for just the basics or add special features that give the word "luxury" new meaning.

Menu Option One: First Class

This is your ideal. This approach will require that you spend time, money, and thought in preparing for it and to do it well. First Class requires a professional quality massage table with a sheepskin pad. The table can also include a heating unit to create warmth under the sheets with 500-count sheets (cotton, percale, satin, or even flannel for those chilly winter nights in the hinterlands) from an expensive department store or catalog. In addition, take the following steps:

❏ Use heavy drapes to block light on your windows.

❏ Find a quiet location, avoiding interruptions or yucky intruding noises; maybe include a cascading waterfall in room—or at least the sounds of one. And don't forget the tunes!

❏ Use oils and plenty of them. Be sure to reread the chapter on oils (Chapter 4) to stock up on your every need. An oil warmer is a lovely way to really get luxurious.

❏ Perfect (dimmed) lighting is a must.

❏ Invest in those thick plush robes to cover you on and off the massage table.

❏ Have a Jacuzzi or hot tub nearby to soothe your aching muscles before or after the massage.

❏ Light the fireplace.

❏ Place a sheepskin rug on the floor for the person giving the massage to stand on.

❏ Stock up on aromatherapy products such as oils, body lotions, and lit candles or diffusers in the room.

❏ Place beautiful images around the room, such as beautiful goddess head statues, O'Keefe paintings, Klimt posters, photos of nature's wonders, or sexy snapshots of the two of you in love.

❏ Grab an eye pillow filled with lavender beads.

Okay. Got the picture yet? This takes spending some bucks on things and really committing to making the setting and your props ready for action.

Menu Option Two: Standard

This is a way to create a great sensual massage, but without having to spend the family fortune on it. Think economical. There's not much distinction between this approach and the next. It's pretty much about how much time, money, and thought you wish to invest:

❏ You can use a futon mattress or your own bed for this one.

❏ Use some of your best sheets, but ones that you don't mind getting a little greasy.

❏ Find some of the leftover candles from the holidays or scoop up some inexpensive ones from your local supermarket on sale.

Finger Tip

Remember that old saw, "What you give you get." The more you put into the experience, the more you will derive benefits. Don't cheat yourself.

❏ As always the basics apply: music (use what you've got), lighting (turn the lights down low or off) and scents (bathe, then sprinkle your favorite cologne on for starters).

❏ We do believe, though, that you must use at least one massage oil if you are going to do this with success. Be creative and find one even at your local discount drug store that can get the job done.

Menu Option Three: Economy

Now we're getting down to the wire for comfort, pleasure, and outcomes that you can count on. This approach will allow you to have a sensual massage that may be more interesting than watching the 11 o'clock news or a football playoff, but it's not going to be all that memorable:

❏ Try lying on a cushy carpet on the floor or a rug where you throw down one of your old sheets.

❏ Grab some pillows for support.

❏ Now oil up with some safflower oil from the cupboard and there you go.

Hang Up Your "Do Not Disturb" Sign

Doing the necessary planning and preparation for a private encounter in your own space may be a bigger challenge than you think. One of the common pitfalls for doing sensual (or any other kind of) massage is interruption. Having quiet, private time and space is essential for sensual massage to be effective. Whether you have a bevy of children, a menagerie of pets, or just a busy life, you need to create the mechanisms for keeping them at bay for just a few hours.

Creating privacy may require some creative thinking on your part. For example, if you have young children, who can you count on to watch them? You may want to reach out to relatives or other parents in a privacy dilemma similar to yours. First show them your copy of *The Complete Idiot's Guide to Sensual Massage*. Second offer to trade off days, in the spirit of good old-fashioned bartering. If they'll watch your little devils on your sensual massage days, you'll watch their little angels on their sensual massage days. A disclaimer: If their little angels turn out to be little devils, you may have to break down and pay for a sitter. If that doesn't work, call on your own parents to pitch in. Maybe say the cat's sick and you need to give it medicine for the next two hours, rather than fess up to your goal of pleasure. The important thing is to make sure your babysitting savior is reliable, so you can relax and enjoy the sensual massage you'll be giving and receiving.

Seven Steps to Privacy

We have found that there are seven basic things you can do to avoid the interruptions that can kill any joy in the sensual massage experience.

- **Make arrangements for the kids and give the dog a big bone.** Send the kids packing to grandma's backyard for a couple of hours, barter with the neighbor to watch them, or schedule your massage when they are in school or at baseball practice. Plan well but get the kids out of there. And keep the animals in their rooms or kennels, even if it breaks your heart for a split second. We mean it. Keep them away from pawing at your pleasure.

- **Shut the windows.** Keep out the distractions of the outer world. Sirens and car crashes don't make for good massage enhancers. Of course, if your home is in a wilderness area or in a quiet neighborhood, open your windows for air!

- **Turn on a fan, heater, or air conditioner to control the flow of air in your space.** You are going to need a comfortable temperature. Anything you can do to prevent discomfort is good.

- **Tell people to leave you alone.** If you have older children, guests, or roommates, hang a sign on your doorknob that signals an unmistakable "Do Not Disturb" message.

- **Turn off all that dratted equipment.** We mean it. No phones, faxes, beeping, or buzzing allowed. Turn on, instead, pleasant background sounds. Play your favorite CD to help block out any distracting sounds, such as the lawn mower in your complex or a garbage truck eating the trash that you threw out so that you could do this sensual massage in the first place!

Finger Tip

Make yourself a "Do Not Disturb" sign to hang on your door. Use it when you and your partner are giving one another massages.

Goddess Helen Says

Enjoying a sensual massage works best when you cut yourself off from the outside world. My husband gets a little nervous if he can't check the caller I.D. to see who's calling, but after our first sensual massage he got the message. Don't destroy the mood by screening calls or leaving the pager on vibrate.

- **Draw the curtains.** Close your curtains, drapes, blinds, or shades. You'd be surprised at how annoying it can be to have a ray of sunlight pierce your eyes when you're trying to give your beloved a rubdown. Even worse than the sun, however, would be the peering eyes of a stranger!

- **Try a natural sound machine.** If outside noise is really a bother, consider recordings that mimic sounds in nature, such as a waterfall or thunderstorm. Take whatever measures are necessary to make your time and space private, quiet, and serene. The unexpected interruption or distraction can ruin the sensual massage experience.

Dr. Patti Says

The most important part of doing sensual massage is setting your intention. Don't get trapped in the thinking that it all has to be perfect. I find that clients sometimes get stuck expecting too much of themselves and their partners, rather than merely saying yes to new adventures. Let yourself set aside time and space for your sensual massage, doing all that you can do to avoid and avert interruptions and disaster, then as they say in the Nike ads, "Just Do It!"

Privacy Check List

We've included the following checklist to help you prepare the environment for your sensual massage and to avert the unwanted event or guest:

- ❏ Have I turned off my cell phone and pager and turned down the volume on my telephone ringer, fax machine, computer, and answering machine?

- ❏ Have I hung my DND sign on the outside doorknob?

- ❏ Have I made arrangements in advance for the kids?

- ❏ Have I tied up or scooted out the pets?

- ❏ Have I left word with my office or family that I am not to be interrupted at this time?

- ❏ Have I purchased a noise-blocking device to take care of unwanted noises?

- ❏ Have I selected the perfect CD?

- ❏ Have I made sure that all the things that I had to take care of so far today are done, like put enough money in the parking meter?

❏ Am I willing to let it all go, even if everything isn't done?

❏ Has my sensual massage partner done all of the above?

If you can't check off most of these items, you may want to postpone this particular sensual massage.

Don't you feel like a master of your environment now? We hope so. This can be an evolving process. You're not going to get all the supplies or enhance your room space to your ultimate liking on the first try. Focus on one sensual massage at a time. Now that you have the idea, make your massage area at home—or on the go—as sensually fulfilling as your imagination will let you.

The Least You Need to Know

◆ Choose the best place in your home for your first sensual massage.

◆ Clean up your space, arrange the furniture, and shut down all your equipment.

◆ Send the kids and pets packing.

◆ Run through the pre-massage checklist to make sure you're ready.

Chapter 11

Seeing Is Believing

In This Chapter

- How eyes affect sensual massage
- Making eye contact
- Having fun with sensual and erotic imagery
- Putting blinders on your blinkers

Seeing is a huge part of sensuality and sexuality, but it's important to keep in mind that people respond to what they see in a variety of different ways. For your sensual massage experience to be one that produces ample pleasure for both partners, you'll need to understand how to take control of what the eyes see. In this chapter, we'll shine the light on several visual issues, including how to be sensitive to lighting in your massage space, how visuals help or hinder the sensual massage process (or the sexual one later on, if you go that far), and how covering the eyes can be used to heighten the other senses.

Seeing Eye-to-Eye

Eye contact is an essential ingredient in feeling connected with your partner. In many esoteric sexual practices, such as *tantric yoga*, which has

Touch Term _____

Tantric yoga is a spiritual tradition from India that focuses on sex as a vehicle for spiritual union and emotional intimacy.

Finger Tip _____

If direct eye contact makes you tense or nervous, just breathe while maintaining an eye contact exchange. Eventually, you will find it easier to do. If emotions surface, let them come up, flow out, and pass by. Don't judge yourself, your partner, or any reactions that either of you may have when sharing an eye-to-eye gaze.

Using eye contact is essential for building your intimacy with a partner. Look deeply into the eyes of your lover, as Gene and Trista show.

(Robert Dunlap)

become quite popular in America, eye-to-eye contact is one of the keys for both sexual and spiritual union. Looking your partner in the eyes can make you feel closer and give you a sense of bonding.

Eye-to eye-contact can be more intimate than sex. Establishing eye contact before your massage builds the connection between you and your partner before any touching begins. Getting closer, feeling more intimate, and even evoking loving emotions can happen through direct eye-to-eye contact. Direct eye contact during a face-up massage can heighten intimacy if sex is on the agenda. It can also be a way to feel more emotionally or spiritually connected to each other.

To create ultimate relaxation during a massage, however, the receiver should close his or her eyes. Sometimes the sheer act of surrendering to a partner's loving touch—without looking—can build trust in a relationship and reestablish a foundation of intimacy that may have been lagging. But just before or after your touch session, making eye contact can really enhance a couple's relationship.

In many spiritual sexual traditions, looking into your lover's left eye with your left eye creates a heart-to-heart connection or feelings of intimacy.

Flipping the Switch

How you light your massage space will set the mood for your sensual massage. Lighting can be used to create almost any kind of mood and ambiance. Just think of the glamorous black-and-white Hollywood photographs of seductress Jean Harlow lying on a bearskin rug. Her innocent white dress reveals just enough skin to whet the observer's appetite, and the dim shadowy lighting lends mystique to the scene, piquing the curiosity and pulling in the viewer. You, too, can create an inviting scene using lighting.

Colored Bulbs and Dimmer Switches

For your sensual massage, don't be afraid to play with light and dark. Doing a massage in the dark, or a very dimly lit space, will force you to rely on your other senses a little more, which can always be fun. Using bright lights in your sensual massage area can create a more clinical setting, something to keep in mind if you want to keep the situation from turning sexual.

If your overhead fixture is hooked to a dimmer, dim away. Dimmed light diffuses, so you avoid the clinical look that bright lights create. Whatever you do, avoid fluorescent lights, as they can be very unflattering.

Finger Tip

To create a romantic glow, don't buy pink bulbs. The rose coloring will make you look pink! Instead, use an amber tint, which will cast a glow that's similar to light at sunset. Sixty-watt amber bulbs in your bedside lamp give you that radiance. If you must use white bulbs, use nothing over 30 watts.

Flickering Candlelight

Or instead of lights, try candles. There's nothing more relaxing and romantic than a room filled with flickering candlelight, the shadows they cast, and the glow of skin in candlelight. Furthermore, lighting a candle symbolizes a special occasion, and you want your massage to be special, right? Experiment with different colored candles. Different colors are associated with different emotions and states of mind, as follows:

Goddess Helen Says

Try spelling out the words "I love you" or form the shape of a heart using tea lights resting in candle-holders or floating on water in lovely bowls. Your candles can also highlight your favorite romantic art or your cherished framed photo of the two of you.

- Red is for passion.

- White is for peace.

- Yellow is for attraction.

- Green is for fertility.

- Light blue is for happiness.

- Pink is for love.

- Orange is for stimulation.

- Purple is for meditation.

Try using candles of different sizes and shapes. The subdued lighting creates a relaxing environment.

Sensual Imagery

Some visual images can get you in the mood for touch. They may take you into a state of openness to share time and space with a sensual massage buddy, or they may open the gateway for more intimate pleasure.

What you see can make you interested in touch, in sex, or it can simply be pleasing to the eyes.

Sexuality Is Subjective

Close your eyes and think of something visually erotic. What did you imagine? A nude man or woman? A graphic depiction of genitalia? A couple in the act of love-making? An alluring, but not graphic, image? Your honey on your wedding day? A teasing glance? A handsome self-portrait? A Calla lily in bloom?

Chances are that what you pictured is different from what your massage partner pictured. That's because what is erotic to Paul may be boring to Phil. Or what is inescapably hot to Susie is repulsive to Sally. As Supreme Court Justice Potter Stewart said about pornography, "I know it when I see it." Well, if one of the top judges in our country can't come up with an objective definition of pornography, neither can we. That means that you get to set your own standards and tastes for what is not only pornographic, but erotic or sexy, to you.

Dr. Patti Says
Research shows that men tend to be more visually-oriented than women. What does that really mean? Men are more likely to be aroused by erotic visual images than are women. Men flip their bic over a half-naked woman posing, or a titillating painting, or suggestive advertising. However, in my own research I found that 40 percent of the video rental and purchase market for porn movies was—are you ready?—women. Either that shows a cultural shift allowing women to enjoy the eye candy of their choosing, or a lot of husbands are using their wives' credit cards without permission!

What Turns You On?

Think about images that may turn you on, or have done so in the past. The list is endless. Here are some ideas to get the creative juices flowing:

- **Past or current lovers.** Think about the first glance, the passionate kisses, making mad love in the moonlight or thrashing about on your comforter for that one forgotten night or a lifetime of loving connection. See it, recalling it with your eyes.

- **A fantasy image.** Think about a sexy movie star, even if it's someone you know in your marrow you are never going to see up close and personally, like Mel Gibson, Catherine Zeta-Jones, Denzel Washington, Britney Spears, or Antonio Banderas. Are you getting the picture yet? They are icons, bigger-than-life images that you get to see up there on the big screen who sometimes you'd like to take home and cuddle or ravage. Conjure up those images to bring you into a state of desire.

- **Adult (XXX) pictures.** If commercial porn or erotica turns you on, that's fine. There are thousands of adult websites, hundreds of nudie magazines, and even live clubs or venues where you can watch women, mostly, perform their hoochie coochie to your heart's content. You can then bring home that wild energy for your sensual massage. If this form of visual entertainment works for you, use it.

- **Erotic art.** There are print and online magazines (our favorite is www. libidomag.com) featuring tasteful, black-and-white imagery that is erotic to a tee. Some art galleries will show their collections of erotic art, if they have any, while others hide it in the back room. There are even art books that contain erotica, such as the Taschen line.

- **Nature.** Think Georgia O'Keefe flower paintings—many of which resemble female sexual anatomy—or photographs of canyons with swooping and curvy lines that ooze out at you, just like the luscious curves of a sexy woman's body. Take the time to see the erotic imagery that abounds in nature.

♦ **Body modification.** There's been a resurgence of interest in ancient practices in the body arts, such as henna inks, tattoos, and even scarification. You may find, as do others, that body mod is a way to show your lover your sexual preferences, or maybe you'll discover the thrill of seeing these decorated bodies on display.

Conjuring up or seeing erotic images may be the spark you need to get started on your sensual massage, or more.

Dr. Patti Says

You may want to try an erotic photo shoot as a way to boost your pleasure potential. Some couples enjoy the process of planning, setting up and taking the photos of each other or themselves as a couple in visually erotic poses. If you have a digital camera, you can take instant pix that capture the moment for you to see right away (if you haven't become distracted too much with touch, that is!). You can also use a video camera to record your most private selves in the buff or in action for your later stimulation. Whatever you choose, making your own personal erotic collection of images may be a great thing to put under your sensual altar (see Chapter 15) or to keep handy for a rainy day designed just for sensual massage.

Out of Sight

Your eyes may get tired, causing stress, fatigue, or lack of interest in looking at anyone or anything. Closing your eyes can rejuvenate even the most tired of souls. We highly recommend using an eye pillow when it's your turn to lie down faceup and take some rubbing. Even a cool slice of cucumber or a wet teabag at room temp or slightly chilled, will soothe your tired eyes.

In addition, sometimes what the eyes *don't* see can be a real turn on! Blindfolding, using either a comfy eye shade (get a better one than those cheap international flights provide, please), a warm washcloth, or even a long silk can be both restorative and evocative for your sensual massage. Finally, erotic blindfolding can be a form of foreplay for sex.

Don't be afraid to experiment with eye coverings during your sensual massage. However, be sure to get your partner's permission before covering her eyes. Just ask politely, and don't be offended if she turns you down. Placing anything over someone else's eyes is delicate business.

Imagine covering up your partner's eyes with a silky eye pillow, as this couple is doing here.

(Robert Dunlap)

If you find this appealing, experiment with various other ways to cover your lover's eyes. Again, if it turns on your light switch, go for it!

The Least You Need to Know

- Just making eye contact with your lover can increase intimacy.
- Invest in good lighting for your sensual massage.
- Erotic images can propel you into sensual massage or more.
- Putting on blinders can make the massage more relaxing, playful, or erotic.

Chapter 12

Listen to This!

In This Chapter

- ◆ The power of sound
- ◆ Choosing music for sensual massage
- ◆ Selecting words to enhance your experience
- ◆ Creating erotic mental images with stories

The fire casts a soft glow on the room, the oil is warm, and your lover is lying naked on a velvet-covered bench, ready to be touched. Sounds perfect, right? Almost, but not quite. If you listen closely, you can hear the whir of the fan and the ticking of the clock, neither of which gets you in the mood for loving touch. You need to add some sensual sounds—music or words—to your environment

Sounds can be distracting, stimulating, stultifying, or soothing. And although some people react more strongly to sound than others, we've all experienced its power in our lives—how the sound of laughter can bring a smile to our faces, a blaring siren can make us wince, or a favorite song can get our feet tap-tap-tapping away. Listen up—it's time bring sound into your massage experience.

The Simple Art of Listening

Imagine the following sounds:

◆ A lawn mower outside your bedroom window

◆ The dishwasher clanking away in the kitchen

◆ Static on the radio

Now imagine these sounds:

◆ Birds chirping in the woods

◆ Your favorite classic musician playing on the radio

◆ Your lover sighing with pleasure

As these two lists demonstrate, what you hear can have a dramatic impact on your sensual massage. Sounds can be soothing or stressful. During a sensual massage, when you are trying to relax and let yourself be one with the moment, sounds can have a particularly strong impact. How loudly you speak, move around the room, what's going on outside the house, and the kind of music that's playing can all affect you.

You or your partner might need music to set a relaxed mood, might respond negatively to outside noises such as a helicopter buzzing overhead, and might need to hear soothing words to guide you into the process.

Tuning In: Music for Mood Making

Music is one of the most powerful tools for creating a sensual atmosphere for your massage. Music has the ability to turn "I'm not in the mood tonight, honey" into "Let's get it on, baby!"

Music can make you laugh and cry. It can bring great joy and deep sadness. And it can heighten the experience of the sensual massage. Scientists have discovered that music has the ability to activate the limbic region in the brain. The limbic region is ultimately responsible for developing your emotions and feelings, such as passion, romance, and nurturing.

Make a Music List

With your partner, make a list of music that puts you both in the mood for romance and keep it with your massage tools. Then next time you give each other massages, pop one of the CDs from your list into the stereo. If you are stuck here because you don't like the same music, take a trip together to a music store that lets you sample music and try to find some mutually enjoyable selections.

Choose music that will complement the mood, not compete with it. Music that is rhythmic is stimulating to the body and has an uplifting effect. Music that is slow and calming to the nerves, with lilting strings and soft pianos, is better for a soothing massage. We do recommend changing your music selection from time to time as your senses become accustomed to the same tunes. Eventually, the familiar songs may no longer spark the fantasy your special moment requires.

Music also stimulates fantasy, which is why great romance movies usually have powerful soundtracks. *Titanic* is a perfect example. Although director James Cameron took home the Academy Award for this film, James Horner's soundtrack helped him win it. Imagine that movie without the glorious voice of Celine Dion crooning, "My heart will go on ..." or the Celtic choirs and symphonic interludes that carry you out to sea.

Humans believe in the power of love, and love is an event discovered through the senses. Music plays an integral part in connecting you with the one you love and inspiring you during sensual massage.

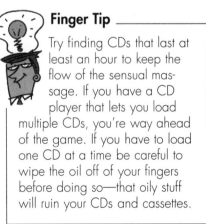

Ouch!

During your sensual massage you don't want to get out of the groove by running out of the tunes. Have at least two hours of music loaded in your player. If you have to interrupt the sensual moment to reload your CD player you may spoil the mood, as well as some great CDs with your oily hands.

Finger Tip

Try finding CDs that last at least an hour to keep the flow of the sensual massage. If you have a CD player that lets you load multiple CDs, you're way ahead of the game. If you have to load one CD at a time be careful to wipe the oil off of your fingers before doing so—that oily stuff will ruin your CDs and cassettes.

Massage Tunes

Here are some suggestions for kinds of music that may enhance your ability to get into the experience more easily, or even intensify what you do or feel during the massage itself:

- Reggae

- New age

- Cool jazz

- Classical

- Romantic ballads

- Celtic rhythms

- Sounds of nature (dolphins, whales, wind, sea)

- Broadway showtunes

- Movie soundtracks

- Lullabies

- Gregorian chants

- Buddhist chants

- Native American flute music

- Drum and bass

- World music

- Sex sounds (CDs that have real sounds of people having sex)

Make up your own list of what you already have in your collection and a "wish list" of those you want to buy.

Choosing Your Words Carefully

What you say affects the energy around and inside of you. For instance, when you speak, you create vibrations. That means that what you say has a physical impact in addition to a mental one. Furthermore, new research shows that using words of praise and healing can alter the shape of water molecules. Negative, critical, harsh, or profane language can create ugly formations in those same water molecules. Amazing science? Yes, particularly if you consider that humans are made up mostly of—you guessed it—water! So if you start to alter what you say and how you speak to your partner, there's a good chance things around you are going to change, too.

Perhaps you read about the studies in which playing classical music helped plants to grow stronger, larger blooms. If a green, growing plant in your living room can have fuller foliage by "listening to" Beethoven, think about how words or sounds may be affecting your ability to blossom in life. Like the plants, you can thrive or die according to what bombards your tender ears. Feed them with healthy, high quality, and life-giving food.

Dr. Patti Says

In the 1980s I had the privilege of attending a workshop run by Gloria Karpinsky, then metaphysical minister and now renowned New Age author. Gloria once demonstrated the power of words in a memorable process. She placed a small pile of metal filings (I think they were iron) on a solid surface. She asked the group to say together the word, "SH#T." As the word was uttered, the magnetic filings formed a black mess. Then she invited us to say aloud the word "LOVE." Amazingly, the filings transformed into a beautiful pattern before our very eyes. That was my first encounter with the vibrational power of language, and I've never forgotten it.

By now we hope you realize the power of your spoken word before, during, or after a sensual massage. Prepping your partner, negotiating who's up first, who does what, and deciding on all of the elements for your time and space all require your attention—and, of course, words. Pay close attention not only to what you say, but how you say it. Words are going to make or break the spell you want to create for your touch time.

Once Upon A Time: Storytelling and Love Tales

Storytelling is an ancient art form that can bring you into a state of relaxation, escape, and pleasure. Maybe you'll want to read aloud from the wells of naughty tales. Such "bedtime" stories can prime the pump for your sensual massage, or after a good rubdown they may be just the lubricant you need to open the gates to a few hours of steamy sex. Telling a juicy story to your sweetheart on the pillows can do more for a sagging sex life than certain blue pills.

Talking sensually or erotically to your partner may be just what's missing to make it take off to another dimension, especially if your ultimate goal is sex. Here are some ideas for how to go about this:

Dr. Patti Says

People who have difficulty feeling their own erotic nature often have trouble creating fantasy for themselves. I often recommend that couples read erotic stories to one another to increase sexual desire. Using erotic stories, in print, on audiotape, or even on videotape can fuel the sexual fires. The hotter the better!

- Pretend you are someone else. Be in a role, as if you were in a play. He's the prince, you're the princess. What would you say to one another?

- Read actual erotic stories aloud. Take a touch break and do a reading, or have a book on tape playing in the background.

- Be you. Dare to talk about what you see, what you feel, what you wish would happen next. Use the act of being present and in the moment and to access that part of yourself and your partner to talk about the two of you your fantasy for doing this sensual massage.

- Talk about the spiritual aspects of your experience. Begin your massage with a ritual (see Chapter 15), then follow it up by playing trance-like music on your CD player, chanting "OM" or other mantras together, and approaching the sensual massage session as a holy encounter with your beloved.

- Raunch it up. Pretend you're in a sleazy hotel or brothel. Your partner is your client. Act like a slutty woman (or guy) who's about to send your client into orbits of pleasure. Tell him or her all about it before you put your hands to work.

Being open to discovery will enhance your sensual massage experience.

The Least You Need to Know

- What you hear can influence how you feel.

- Music is a powerful tool in your sensual massage.

- Make what you say during a sensual massage count.

- Don't be afraid to share your fantasies with your partner.

Chapter 13

Mmmm ... Smells Good, Tastes Great

In This Chapter

- ◆ All about essential oils
- ◆ Aromatherapy and its origins
- ◆ Flowers can say it all
- ◆ Edible sensual treats
- ◆ Having fun with food

Ever walk by a bakery and have the smell of warm chocolate chip cookies or the aroma of fresh baked bread trigger memories of grandma's house? Or does the smell of a certain aftershave cologne take you back to high school and the guy who got away? Imagine life without the scent of exotic perfumes, roasted coffee beans, or freshly cut grass. Perhaps more than any other sense, smell can transport you to your past just from a passing whiff. Harnessing the power of smell for your sensual massage by using carefully selected essential oils, lighting aromatic candles, or even setting up your table by the ocean's salty spray can evoke ecstasy.

Makes Scents to Me

It wasn't until 1937 that the French chemist Rene Maurice Gattefosse coined the term "aromatherapy," although people had recognized the healing properties of aromatic plants for centuries. Aromatherapy uses essential oils (the liquid that is present in tiny droplets or sacs) from plants for the purpose of healing. An essential oil is what gives a rose its fragrance.

When essential oils are inhaled through the nasal passages or absorbed through the skin they travel to the limbic region of the brain, which is responsible for memory and emotion.

Once you open yourself up to your emotions, there's no telling what can happen. Those open, warm, juicy feelings of closeness or soft gentle vulnerabilities may be all you need to be perfectly attuned for a tender touch exchange.

As noted in Chapter 4, you can purchase essential oils from your local health store and add them to your carrier oil for your sensual massage. The type of essential oil that you choose will determine the outcome: You can choose oils that are stimulating and invigorating or oils that are soothing and relaxing. The following table lists some properties of common and not-so-common essential oils.

Essential Oils and Their Properties

	Aphrodisiac	Calming	Cleansing	Sedative	Soothing	Stimulating	Warming
Cedarwood			✓			✓	
Chamomile		✓	✓		✓		
Cinnamon			✓				
Clary sage				✓			✓
Clove			✓				✓
Cypress				✓			
Eucalyptus			✓				
Frankincense		✓					
Jasmine	✓		✓			✓	
Lavender		✓		✓			
Orange				✓			
Patchouli	✓		✓				
Peppermint						✓	

	Aphro-disiac	Calming	Cleansing	Sedative	Soothing	Stimu-lating	Warming
Rose	✓	✓	✓		✓		
Rosemary							
Sandalwood	✓	✓			✓	✓	
Tea tree			✓				
Wintergreen						✓	✓
Ylang ylang	✓			✓	✓		

Essential oils are highly volatile, meaning that they easily evaporate. Store them in dark glass containers away from direct sunlight. They should not be used directly on the skin as they are potent and could irritate it. Always use them blended with a carrier oil by placing 5 to 15 drops of essential oil into 1 ounce of carrier oil.

Synergy

Essential oils can also be blended together, which is known as a synergy. One of our favorite blends for sensual massage is jasmine and ylang ylang, equal parts of each. The jasmine is stimulating and the ylang ylang is soothing and sedative. For a calming effect, lavender is always the best, in combination with orange oil. To create a stimulating result, pour equal amounts of peppermint and rosemary oils into a diffuser for burning.

If romance or sex is your goal, then here are three special "love potions" to get you in the mood. For an aphrodisiac massage combo, use anything with rose or ylang ylang, especially to ignite the fires in women. Put a few drops of each in a bowl of warm water, a diffuser, or over a candle stand for at least 20 minutes in the room before you begin your massage. Another love treat is made by placing a few drops each of jasmine, rose, sandalwood, and bergamot in a carrier oil for the massage itself. Finally, you can add 10 drops of each ylang ylang, jasmine, sandalwood, patchouli, and clary sage into your bath to enhance your readiness for romance.

What's Your Favorite?

Discuss with your partner the smells you both like and associate with sensuality. Visit your local health food store (or look in Appendix B for suggested online and mail order outlets) and pick out the scents you both like. Don't make the mistake of massaging your partner with rose oil if he would prefer a woodsy aroma like sandalwood or green fir. Consider the following scents:

- Musky scents, such as sandalwood, patchouli, anything woodsy, or pure musk itself

- Natural citrus smells, such as lemon, orange or grapefruit

- Nutty odors (this is not a judgment call about your mental health), such as coconut, sesame, or almond

- Flowery scents, such as rose, lilac, jasmine, or perfumed blends

- Odorless oils, a pure carrier oil like grape seed or professional massage oil base

- Aphrodisiac oils, such as the commercial preparations sold by Kama Sutra or other brands, or jasmine or ylang ylang oils

- Sporty oils, such as wintergreen, rosemary, or eucalyptus

Finger Tip

Take a handful of coffee beans with you to the store when you're shopping for essential oils. Sniffing the beans in between sniffing the different aromas will clear the nose.

Aromatherapy Tips

If you want to enhance the smell of your massage area but don't want to apply the oil to your body, you can try any of the following aromatherapy ideas:

- Drop 5 to 15 drops of essential oil in your bath water, making sure it is blended into the water by swishing the water with your hand before sinking in and soaking.

- Buy aromatherapy candles or add one to two drops of essential oil to the melting wax of a nonscented candle.

- Drip some oil in a room diffuser, which converts the oil to a fine spray and directs it around the room.

- Add a few drops to your final rinse when washing your clothes.

- Drizzle a few drops onto the towels or spray the sheets you are going to use for your sensual massage, adding six to eight drops to one ounce of purified water. You can use the same water as a mister, which you can gently spray into the air during your massage when you turn your partner over. Lavender and rose are good blends, or synergies, to use here.

- Add 5 to 10 drops in a small bowl of warm water and place it on a radiator, allowing the heat to release the scents.

Perfume Your Way to Pleasure

Perfumes have the same effect as essential oils on the limbic region of your brain, especially if you associate the perfume with romantic or emotionally uplifting memories. So why not dab some on before your sensual massage? You can decide which perfume is a perfect reflection of you.

You can create your own perfume from essential oils. Not only will you smell luscious, you'll feel better, breathe easier, and be more alert.

Dr. Patti Says
Sexual attraction is often triggered by pheromones, or mating chemicals, that animals—including humans—secrete. Researchers have conducted studies in which they showed women pictures of men on a screen. Without the women knowing, the researchers released the pheromone-rich underarm sweat of men while some pictures appeared on the screen. Now get this: Time after time, when the sweat was present, the women found themselves attracted to the men pictured on the screen. And you thought that sweating was a bad thing?

A Rose by Any Other Name

The gift of flowers is a wonderfully romantic gesture. And did we mention that few things smell better than freshly cut flowers? A bouquet of blossoms in a beautiful vase will enhance your massage space by adding aroma, romance, and color.

There are other ways, too, in which flowers can enhance your experience. If you and your partner bathe in preparation for your sensual massage (see Chapter 17), carefully pick the petals from a rose and sprinkle them into the water to indulge the colors and essences. Or leave a trail of petals leading to your massage area for your partner to find, symbolizing a pathway to pure pleasure. Arrange an outline of a heart with petals on your massage altar (see Chapter 15). Shower petals on the massage sheets so that your loved one lies on the soft bed of petals. (We recommend that you use dark sheets as the rose petals can stain the sheets, especially if they get massage oil on them. Or you can brush them off once your honey has had the delicious visual image of them.)

 Finger Tip

Ask your florist to save you a bag of rose petals (as they often pick off the petals to extend the life of the flower and would otherwise throw them away) to incorporate into your next massage experience.

More Scintillating Scents

Now that we've opened you up to the power of smells, here's an activity you can try, either with your partner or on your own. Read over the following list of scents. Try to imagine their smell and how that smell makes you feel (open, happy, excited, pleased, aroused, heated up, interested). This exercise will help you to determine what kinds of scents to use during your sensual massage.

Hot chocolate	Your dog's paws
Peanut butter	Lavender massage oil
Freshly cut grass	New leather
Shalimar perfume	Summer rainfall
Spaghetti sauce	A pine forest
Fresh mown hay	Suntan lotion
A slice of lemon	Perfumed hand soap
A spruce tree branch	Your lover's shampoo
Freshly brewed coffee	Lilac blossoms
Crackling logs on the fire	Dirty underwear
Strawberries	Body odor
Seaweed	Just-out-of-the-oven cookies

Stimulated yet? Choose the scents that appeal most to you—and don't censor yourself! It's okay if the smell of your lover's grungy workout gear turns you on. Don't be afraid to use that smell for your nasal aphrodisiac or sensual massage prelude.

Food for Thought

We've already talked about the aromatic power of some foods. However, you may want to go beyond just smelling some foods, and actually tantalize your partner's taste buds with them. Perhaps you already are thinking chocolate? We are! If the taste of chocolate can send shivers of enjoyment into your nose, just think what it can do when you place a morsel of dark chocolate on his or her tongue? Or how about some coconut to evoke thoughts of tropical islands and South Seas romance?

Think about some of your favorite foods or beverages and make a list of them. Then go shopping and fill your cart with an array of foods that you and your partner will be able to savor as part of your sensual massage. Use this lip-smacking stop on the road to sensual pleasure as preparation for or as part of your sensual massage. Shopping lists ready?

Sharing sensual foods with your lover may be the path to more pleasure.

(Robert Dunlap)

If you enjoy sweets, pull some cookies and persimmons off the shelf, or if you prefer salty foods, go for salted nuts and beef jerky. Of course, different kinds of foods go great together—why do you think chocolate (sweet) bars with peanuts (salty) taste so good? So try to include a variety of foods—salty, sweet, sour, and even bitter. Here are some ideas to get those creative juices flowing, brought to you from your four taste centers on the tongue:

- ◆ **Sweet:** chocolate Kisses, peach torte, fresh strawberries, honey
- ◆ **Sour:** cranberry juice, lemons, and vinegar

- **Salty:** pretzels, salted nuts, kippered fish, beef jerky, salted rim for that margarita
- **Bitter:** dark chocolate, pomegranate, blood oranges, citrus peels

Use these foods and drinks to power your motors! Remember, sensual massage takes energy to do. A little fueling now and then will help give you the strength and inspiration to keep going. The aromas and tastes will awaken your senses before, during, and after a sensual massage. Even an after-massage snack or taking breaks before switching roles will prolong the sensual ecstasy through your taste.

And by the way, when you are actually sharing skin-to-skin touch and allowing yourself to surrender to the sensual massage process, you may be surprised to find that you are more open to exploring new taste preferences than before. Hmmmm, or rather, mmmmm.

Without a Trace

In addition to eating your food, you can have some fun with it. Pick out some food with textures, temperatures, and tastes that you think your partner will enjoy. Ask your partner to lie down (faceup), close his or her eyes, and focus on his or her lips. Using the food you've picked out, trace around those luscious lips.

Ideas include:

Chocolate or butterscotch sauce, warmed up or refrigerated

Tapioca pudding

Vanilla massage oil (edible)

Whiskey

Red wine

Honey

Cake frosting

Butter

Ice cubes

Grape juice

Cranberry sauce

To apply the food, you can use your finger or even textured items like a BBQ or pastry brush, or even a body part that you find particularly sensual. Keep in mind that doing this might arouse your partner (wink, wink).

Dr. Patti Says

Did you ever wonder what makes the lips so sensuous—so responsive to touch? If you drag a textured cloth across your lips, you notice right away how sensitive they are. Physical sensations happen in the lips thanks to the Meisner's corpuscles, sensitive nerve fibers found in the lips.

Aside from the nerve sensations, get this: A kiss is the beginning of the sexual response cycle in humans, which starts with the triggering and then the dumping of chemicals throughout the hormone chain in the human body. No wonder lips are so sexy.

The Least You Need to Know

- ◆ The sense of smell can provoke deep memories.
- ◆ There are a variety of essential oils on the market, each with unique properties.
- ◆ Aromatherapy can be used during a massage to achieve the desired mood.
- ◆ Foods can evoke a sensual response.

Part 4

Beyond Touch

You already know that people use massage to satisfy a variety of needs—that's one of the amazing thing about touch! But it's important that you and your massage partner know what you each wants out of the experience. If you don't make your intentions clear up front, you run the risk of failing to satisfy one or even both of you. This section will talk you through the process of deciding your goals for each massage and discussing those goals with one another. You'll also learn the key components of what we like to call "body talk"—using nonverbal cues to communicate with your partner.

There's no doubt that massage can lead to greater intimacy, but only if you're able to open yourself up to the experience. We'll point out potential emotional obstacles to intimacy and what you can do to overcome them. Once you open yourself up to all that massage has to offer, it can be a spiritual experience. The final chapter in this section will explore how to harness those good vibes.

Chapter 14

Communication Is Key

In This Chapter

- ◆ Who goes first and for how long
- ◆ Making your intentions clear
- ◆ Giving and receiving feedback
- ◆ Opening up to the power of massage

This chapter will help you to navigate the sometimes smooth and other times choppy waters of communicating about massage. We'll talk you through some foundational things such as who goes first (a rather basic building block, wouldn't you say?), as well as more abstract concepts such as what you both want to get out of the experience and how you would like it to unfold. We're not talking about fluffing the towels here, but the process of who does what, what's okay and what's not okay, and how far you both want to go.

Remember earlier when we said that the purpose of massage can be for healing, pleasure, relaxation, or foreplay? Well, this is your chance to decide for yourself and then make your intentions clear with your partner. "What the heck am I doing this for?" is a question that you really want to answer before you start applying the oil. If you are one of those couples who are already very keen on each other, or madly in lust, or dripping with chemistry, this is a no-brainer—you know that your massage session is going to lead to sex. But maybe you're newcomers to the relationship, just friends, or even barely know each other's name (fine by us, by the way), and the last thing on your minds is anything more intimate than a good backrub.

We encourage you to go through all of the activities in this chapter, get clear on your intentions, and then go for what you *really* want.

> ### Goddess Helen Says
>
> Think of each sensual massage as a unique journey to somewhere new. Like the geography of Ireland or Wales, each hill and valley of your lover's body will be special with each visit. Think like a geographer and you're going to find more joy each time you travel.

Who's On First?

You are about to hit the dance floor of touch, and one of you has to take the lead. It's time to choose which partner you want to be. One of you has to be the giver and the other lucky duck gets to be receiver. If you cannot decide, then flip a coin. If that's not enough, then draw a card and pick the highest suit. If that's not enough, then look in the back of this book for Dr. Patti's office number and book a couples' coaching appointment to resolve your major communication block. Seriously, folks, this shouldn't be difficult.

When, Where, and How Many?

If you haven't selected the best place to play lay-me-down yet, it's time to do that. Is it going to be on the dining room table, do you need to set up that new professional massage table, or are you at the beach and planning to throw down a sleeping bag? Consider rereading Chapter 10, then choose a place that suits you both and take your positions.

But before you strip off those work clothes or even lock the door, take a minute to determine how much time you can devote to today's session. Do you each want a half hour massage to start? Or is this an all day thing? Be sure to make it fair and even up the time allocations. It's perfectly okay if one of you chooses to receive touch today and the other gets her delight tomorrow night, for example. You can get creative here, as long as you decide beforehand how long this is going to go and who does what. Got it yet?

What's In It for Me?

Now that we have the simple stuff out of the way, it's time to take it to the next level: Determining your goals for this particular massage session.

Read over the following list of reasons why you might want to receive a massage. Use it as a guide for where you'd like your upcoming session to lead. Ask your partner to do the same. Identifying your reasons for wanting a massage will help to open the lines of communication and boost intimacy, and it will also get you in the right mood. If there is a great discrepancy between your goals, it's probably time to put down the oils and grab a cup of java.

❑ You just want to have a human touch your body, anywhere, anyhow, anything. It's been months or years.

❑ You simply want to relax, forget about your worries, and just get comfortable.

❑ You have been through a rough time physically lately. Maybe you're recovering from an illness, surgery, or a baby, or medications are getting you down. You could really use some healing touch right now to soothe you and help you release some of those toxins and bad tensions.

❑ You've been overworking it in the gym and feeling a little sore. Your muscles are screaming for a good rubdown.

❑ You want to have your senses awakened.

❑ You want to create more intimacy in your new relationship.

❑ You're in a long-term relationship and are looking to rekindle your intimacy.

❑ You're in it for the sexual foreplay, plain and simple.

There's no need to actually get out this book and review this list every time you begin a massage, but we do encourage you do discuss your intentions with your partner each and every time you begin a massage. After all, nobody can read your mind. You may be surprised to learn that Harry has a headache or that Susie's day was too horrendous to take any more touching than the equivalent of a cup of sedative tea. Talk to your partner and you both will discover your boundaries. By the way, the more open you are about your intentions, the more likely you will be to engage in massage because you will feel comfortable with each other.

Also remember that you can change your goals every time you decide to give one another a massage. Just because for this very session you decide you want your massage to serve as foreplay, for instance, doesn't mean that every massage must lead to sex.

Dr. Patti Says

I often find that for married couples who have gone stale in the bedroom, getting into a new pattern helps to cure what ails them. For example, one couple I worked with rediscovered their libidos when they went to a nude weekend workshop on sensual massage at a local spa retreat. Once there, they discovered a new way to touch. The ambience of seeing other people naked around them helped to give them fresh perspectives on their sensuality, adding to their playful connection. Their faces glowed when they talked about how much they opened up.

Rules of the Road: Body Talk Principles

You can communicate how you're feeling during a massage without actually uttering a word. We call this practice body talk, and it's a means of communication that you'll become very fluent in if you make massage a regular part of your life.

The body talks to you as you massage it. The muscles you touch talk back to you. When you are focused on your partner and really want to give her as much pleasure as possible, her body will guide your moves—it will tell you what areas are painful even if she doesn't know the source of the discomfort. Simply explore every area of her body, persuading the muscles to reveal their needs.

 Finger Tip

A tight muscle, like a drum skin, is hard to lift with your fingers. It is telling you that it needs a little more attention, and it will respond with gratitude when you gently knead it. A relaxed muscle can easily be lifted from the bone.

Body talk involves being aware of your partner during the massage. It means being sensitive to her needs and utilizing your five senses to fulfill those needs. If you are aware and in the moment, you will see your partner's muscles melting. Watch as the grimace on her face is replaced with a smile.

No More Monkey-See, Monkey-Do!

It's easy to play monkey-see, monkey-do. We know that you could have read a therapeutic massage cookbook—those how-to guides that offer a cookie cutter approach to massage without acknowledging that we each have unique needs and that those needs and desires change every time we engage in massage. Are you going to fulfill your intentions simply by imitating some massage moves? A great massage, especially a sensual one, is all about awareness. Your intention is to bring pleasure and comfort to your partner. The moment you have started following a massage cookbook, you have left the flow of the moment.

The language of touch is so natural that it doesn't require an interpreter. Your thoughts and intuitive awareness can be your guides. In fact, much like a blind person can read Braille lettering, your hands can read the relaxed and tense spots of your partner's body. If you're focused on reading your partner's body, it will guide your every move.

> **Goddess Helen Says**
>
> Intimate body talk is like shared laughter: It brings you together. Even massaging your partner's hand can be a sensually fulfilling event all its own, caressing around and between the fingers and gently rubbing the soft pillow side of the palm.

Let Your Fingers Do the Talking

Body talk is a two-way form of communication. Not only can you, as the giver of the massage, understand your partner's needs by "listening" to her muscles, but also you can send messages back to her through those fingers and hands of yours. The types of strokes you use, the pace of your movements, the amount of pressure you apply— these are all forms of bodily communication. Be sure you send the right messages.

With your hands and your thoughts, you can take your partner anywhere your heart desires. Maybe your partner has been going through some bad times and you want to reassure him that everything is going to be okay. To do this, think positive and healing thoughts as you stroke him. Your reassuring touch will fill him with a sense of calm, elevate the experience of pleasure, and hasten the healing.

If during your massage a negative thought enters your mind, think to yourself, "Cancel that." Otherwise, your partner will pick up on that negativity.

> **Ouch!**
>
> You can transfer emotions through your hands. If you are angry, depressed, or otherwise emotionally upset, don't give someone a massage—you'll risk transferring those negative emotions to your partner. Instead, ask your partner for a rain check. Trust us, there's nothing worse than a halfhearted effort or sending negative energy to your partner's receptive body.

The Feedback Loop of Likes and Dislikes

We encourage you to be silent and communicate through body talk as much as possible. As the giver, make sure that you aren't doing too much with your mouth—talking, that is—rather than "sensing" how it's going. There's nothing worse than, as the person getting the rubdown, being jolted out of a comfortable trance by your partner's loud "How'm I doing so far?" Instead of checking in with your voice, use your hands as your eyes and ears. Let your hands tell you if he's flinching a muscle or relaxing into your movements. Don't keep interrupting the physical process with words. Let it all flow, better in silence than with speaking.

Finger Tip

At the beginning of your massage, gently ask your partner, "Is that enough pressure or too much?" Use your partner's response to determine how much pressure to use for the rest of the rubdown.

However, there are times when you should feel free to speak up, especially if you are the receiver and something is painful or making you uncomfortable. Don't be afraid to tell your partner whether the oil or her hands are too cold or that she's tapping too hard. And if something feels particularly good, go ahead and moan with pleasure and a whispered "oh … yessss." The feedback loop of likes and dislikes has to be open. That's part of the secret for a successful sensual massage.

There are times, too, when the person giving the massage will need to check in. This is an opportunity to get instant feedback about what you are doing and how it's affecting your mate. He may appear to be bothered by your stroke, pressure, or movement. Gently and quietly, lean in and ask in your most in-a-sacred-mosque of a voice, "Is that okay?" or "Too much pressure?" or "Am I hurting you?"

The partner receiving the massage can whisper a quick "yes," "no," "more," "ouch," or "stop!" Or you can work out some hand signals ahead of time, such as the following:

- To show that something is painful, make a fist.

- To show that something feels good, open your palm.

- To show that something feels ticklish, jiggle your hand.

- To show that you want more pressure, put your hand on her leg with some pressure.

Dr. Patti Says

If there is one thing that saves marriages, business partnerships, families, and tribes, it is the ability to listen. Listening is both a learned skill and an art form. Doing a sensual massage will require that you be a good listener before, during, and after the massage.

Here is a technique that may help you to become a better listener:

Get an egg timer, set it for three minutes, and sit down with your partner. Flip a coin, and have whoever wins the toss be Partner A and whoever loses be Partner B. Have Partner A talk about a problem he or she's having until the timer goes off. Next, set the timer for one minute. Partner B should summarize what he or she heard Partner A say until the timer again goes off. Partner B should then ask Partner A, "Did I understand you correctly?" Partner A can offer some clarifications if necessary.

Now, switch roles and repeat the process. When you both have finished, discuss for a set time, such as 10 or 15 minutes, any solutions to the problems you brought up. Use your timer if necessary. Focus like a laser beam on the issues that surface, and try to come up with real solutions and not on belaboring the problems. This simple process, repeated weekly, can transform your relationship, your sensual massage potential, and even your sense of peace.

Open Your Parachute

We believe that sensual massage can be a gateway to self-expansion and self-discovery, leading you to places inside yourself that you never before knew existed. But for that to happen, you have to open yourself up to the possibilities and give yourself over to the moment.

Some ideas that may help you get the most from massage include the following:

◆ Be willing to experiment; try new things.

◆ Leave your critic at the door; avoid self-judgment.

◆ Let go of your old boundaries; release your old ways of thinking about and doing things.

◆ Release yourself from expectations; even if you can choose an outcome, remove all expectations for good or bad results.

◆ Avoid disappointment; if you can accept that whatever happens may be a joyful ride, go with it.

◆ Go free; learn how to "free fall," like unfurling your parachute, letting yourself really go.

Most of all, enjoy yourself, and share your feelings with your partner!

The Least You Need to Know

◆ Communication is a foundation for doing sensual massage.

◆ Be clear about your intentions before you begin.

◆ Giving feedback to your partner is essential.

◆ You can communicate without words.

Catch the Spirit

In This Chapter

◆ What is chi and how to enhance it

◆ How to focus on the moment

◆ All about tantra

◆ The power of rituals

◆ Creating your own sacred altar

Spirituality might be a lot harder to grasp than a claw roller and a bottle of coconut oil, but it's just as real. And the spiritual benefits of sensual massage can be just as powerful as the physical sensations of a good rub-down.

Get ready to explore the spirituality of touch. You may find yourself taken into the realm of your spirit by reading about (then trying) the ancient practices of conscious breathing, or discover that you really want to learn more about tantra, or even start engaging in rituals with your partner. It's all up to you. We suggest that you read this chapter, think about it and let the ideas settle into your soul, and then choose what pulls at your innermost self. This is a chapter designed to take you to that special place inside of you, that space of personal uniqueness and oneness that you find when you dedicate yourself to going inward. Ready? Here we go, down, down, down ....

The Chi of Life

There are many words for the energy of life. We call it chi, others call it the ki, and still others identify it as spirit, soul, or even White Feather. You may think of it as God. You may think of it simply as the flow of life. You may not think about it at all, until you see a field of lavender in the south of France and go, "Wow, how did that get there?" It really doesn't matter what you call it, as long as you can recognize it within yourself and other living creatures in the world. Whenever you are aware that you are alive and exist in a world inhabited by other living things, you're tapping into the source of life, or chi.

In Eastern medicine, chi governs health. Where chi flows, health is. If your chi gets blocked, then you get sick, weak, or stagnate. Many people believe that chi stagnation can lead to serious disease and eventually even death—not something to take lightly. But the opening of chi can feel as light as air or as heavy as lead, depending on what you do about it and what form you use.

Often the words "chi" or "ki" are associated with spiritual, healing, or martial arts practices. One of these is tai chi, a form of spiritual practice that uses body movements to take you into that flow of chi moving around and through you. Using feet and hand movements, even postures, you can feel the life force energy moving as you move your body. A healing massage practice involving chi is called Reiki, which literally means "life force energy." This healing art form uses a transference of energy through the hands to create a balancing of the body's energies. One of the loveliest forms of martial arts also relies on chi. It is called Aikido, and it uses the principles of taking the energy from one person, including an assailant, and circling it back to that person. It's a true metaphor for the giving/receiving circle of life, or in this case, sensual massage. The sheer act of laying hands on another human being and moving them along the body activates chi for both giver and receiver. Sensual massage, like tai chi and other spiritual practices, gets your chi going.

Mind Over Matter

To do anything well, you must focus on it. The same goes for sensual massage, particularly if you want to connect with your chi, life energy, spirit, or whatever else you want to call it. If you experience a lot of "inner chatter" or find that it's difficult to pay attention to what you're doing for more than a few minutes, you won't be able to get into the moment of the massage. It's only when you get into the moment, focus only on the activity at hand, and forget all your worries and cares, that you will be able to connect with your chi and your partner and truly have a spiritual experience.

Focus In

The following exercise teaches you how to use an imaginary object for your point of focus. Once you get practiced at doing this, you can transfer what you learn to any task, such as focusing on giving a spectacular sensual massage to that lovely woman sitting on the sofa in front of you right now.

Here's how: Read our instructions for focusing on a gold coin, then practice focusing on the coin for about five minutes. If you cannot do it without losing concentration, leave it alone for a while, come back to it later, and try it again.

Here we go:

Imagine a gold coin in the palm of your right hand. (If you are left-hand-dominant, you may want to use that hand instead.) Now, close your eyes, and really feel that coin lying there in your hand. Allow it to heat up. Concentrate on that very spot where the imaginary coin is sitting on your hand. Send heat to it. Let it get very hot. If you wish, you can also start out with an actual coin, just to get the sensations going.

If you felt a lot of warmth, that's great. Even if you only produced a tiny amount of lukewarm sensation, you are on your way to mastering the technique of mental focusing. Don't give up! You can do this little exercise each day to hone your mental focusing skills.

Prana High

You can use your breathing to help you focus. Directed breathing, or *pranayama*, is an ancient technique that is widely practiced today. If done correctly, you can use it to quiet the chatter of the mind (sometimes known as "monkey mind") and become centered in the here and now.

Touch Term _____

Pranayama is a directed breathing technique drawn from sacred Indian scripture. It involves concepts of restraint, life, and death.

You can try pranayama on your own. Sit quietly. Put your thumb over one nostril and inhale deeply. Hold your breath for a four count; then release your exhaling breath while pressing with your third finger on the other nostril. Continue this pattern slowly for about five minutes. You'll be amazed at how clearly you can focus and how it also cleans out those cobwebs in your brain!

Feel Your Thoughts

Once you're focused, you're ready for the next step: *feeling*. This will help you stay in the present moment and not worry about "what next." Feel all of your emotions and thoughts (yes, you read that right, we said *feel* your thoughts.) As spiritual teacher Ernest Holmes taught, "Thoughts are things." Treat them as things. Feel all the sensations pulsating through your mind at this very moment. And don't forget to keep breathing. Breathing with consciousness helps to get and then keep you in the moment.

> **Finger Tip**
>
> Check out the website www.ajourneyintonow.com, which is all about how to access and remain in the moment. Or try reading (or listening to the taped recording of) *The Power of Now*, a bestseller by Eckhart Tolle. It's probably the single most powerful teaching on how to make the most of the present.

So what's focus got to do with sensual massage? Plenty. Focus is one of the foundations for sensual touch. To be a good giver of touch you must learn to focus on what you are doing, as you also learn to focus on the present moment. As a receiver, putting your focus on all of those feel-good sensations is going to help you find the pleasure in sensual touch. By the way, that same message applies to good sex: keep your attention on the positive sensations, and you are going to last longer and experience more pleasure as a couple delighting in skin to skin.

Body Temple Arts

In some traditions, especially in those ancient ones from India, the home of the *Kama Sutra* and of tantric yoga, the genitalia are given sacred spiritual names. The name for the vulva (which includes the clitoris, vagina, labia, and all the inner parts of the woman's sexual anatomy) is referred to as "yoni." The male counterpart, especially the penis, is referred to as "lingham." The philosophy of tantric sexuality teaches that when yoni and lingham unite, ecstasy is possible—even enlightenment or oneness with God. If, that is, you believe in that path. Tantra is not for everyone, although you may find claims as such.

We believe that it's a wonderful spiritual path, a path to sexual bliss, even spiritual awakening to enlightenment, but it's not a cure-all. Tantra is a way to find harmony, union, and enhance your intimacy along with your sexual pleasure. Much like the *Kama Sutra*, that ancient lovemaking manual, tantric yoga is a guide, not a gospel. If the sound of Sanskrit, wearing toe rings, or breathing in synchrony while holding a sacred sexual pose entwined in your lover's arms calls to you, then tantra may be for you.

> **CAUTION**
>
> **Ouch!** _____
>
> Be careful about legitimate practitioners of the sacred sexual arts. There are some really good ones out there (see Appendix B for a few recommendations) and a few who are not authentically tantric masters or guides. Ask around for a referral or go to www.tantra.org for the real deal—it shows the depth of what tantric traditions and practices are really all about, from experts, not fakes who want to part you from your hard-earned dollars for the sake of titillation.

Rites of Passage

We are ritual junkies. Over the many years in which we have practiced our professions, helped thousands of people, and taken our own personal journeys, we have discovered the power of using ritual in daily life. Rituals change things. Rituals bring different intentions and special energies to whatever you do. Rituals are a way for you to make each day special. Remember in those Elizabethan times, when the lord would drip his red wax on his decree and then seal it with his letter stamp before sending off his special message to the world? You do that, too, through your rituals.

You may be surprised to learn that you are already doing rituals. Here are some areas of your daily life to consider as possible rituals, things that you do in your own certain way each time:

- How you answer the phone
- How and where you eat your dinner
- How you greet strangers
- How you fold the newspaper
- How you say good night to your honey
- How you sign off in an e-mail

Do you see the importance of ritual in your life?

We suggest and encourage you to try some special rituals as a prelude to your sensual massage. If you already have a ritual you have developed together, good for you! If not, consider giving the following honoring ritual a try.

Honoring Ritual

The honoring ritual is a wonderful ceremony for—you guessed it—honoring a loved one. It involves telling your partner why you appreciate him (or her) and that you honor his presence. If you are feeling creative, you can even write something in honor of your lover. Don't rely on trite expressions of greeting card fluff here—this is your chance to mention specific things about your partner that you appreciate. Maybe you like the way your partner has a meal ready for you after a long day at work, or the fact that he or she is always willing to listen—*really listen*—to your problems. You may honor the way your partner makes you laugh or even a little thing like the way she calls out to you when you come home. Talk about how these actions or characteristics make you feel. Don't hold back!

Sit facing each other on the floor in a comfortable position wearing loose, relaxed clothing, or no clothing at all. Be natural and hold hands if you like. Close your eyes and start breathing deeply yet softly through the nose, letting your belly, ribs, and chest expand to full capacity. Then exhale all the air through your nose until your belly is pressed against your spine. Repeat this breathing until you both feel a sense of calmness. Take turns honoring one another with your words. Relish the ritual as you might savor water after a long walk. Once you've completed the ritual, you'll be focused on one another and ready to begin your massage.

> **Goddess Helen Says**
>
> Rituals give you the chance to celebrate the big and little things you appreciate in each other. Cherish each other through ritual, and, of course, sensual massage.

The Altar of Sensual Delights

One way to help you treat each and every sensual massage as a sacred act is to set up an altar in your massage space devoted to massage and its sensual delights. This will serve as a reminder of the spiritual side of sensual massage, and it may help you to get into the right mood and to get focused.

Decorate a table, nightstand, or dresser with a beautiful covering—a large silk scarf or tapestry, for example. Display trinkets, mirrors, and romantic photos of you and your partner on the altar. Place crystals and gemstones or other meaningful items around the altar area. Adorn the walls and rooms with artful paintings or statuettes of lovers, provocative posters, and other objects that arouse the senses. When you do the massage, bring in fresh fruit, sweet scented candles and flowers to enhance the presence of your altar. The more sensuality, the better!

Design your own sensual altar to enhance your intimacy and spiritual connection. This is how Kevin and Martha Ellen are deepening their bond.

(Robert Dunlap)

Your altar is a place that evokes and reinforces your sacred side. It can also deepen your connection to your loved one. You can look at your altar each day as a reminder of all the benefits you feel from sharing sensual touch. It's the perfect way to recreate feelings of oneness, harmony, and peace that sensual massage creates and that put you in the mood for more.

Finger Tip

Make ritual a part of your sensual massage.

The Least You Need to Know

◆ Chi flow is essential to your health.

◆ Mental discipline may be your best ally.

◆ Directed breathing can help you focus.

◆ Your rituals carry you through your life.

Chapter 16

Bonding and Intimacy

In This Chapter

◆ Understanding intimacy

◆ Identifying and overcoming barriers to intimacy

◆ Getting intimate with you and your partner's body

◆ Giving in to the act of receiving

Sensual massage can be a prelude to intimacy. It can be a more intimate experience than sexual intercourse itself! At the same time, many of our clients have stated that taking off their clothes for a hands-on rubdown can produce more sweat from the sheer anxiety of being touched than a four-hour workout at the gym. Plus, they sweat bullets at the thought of baring it all—their bodies *and* their emotions—to their massage partner.

In this chapter we're going to teach you about intimacy and about opening yourself up so that you can better connect with yourself and your partner. But before we talk about the actual laying on of hands, let's take a look at the foundation of intimacy.

Note: While parts of this chapter may sound like a crash course in psychology or something straight out of a self-help manual, trust us: If you feel better about yourself, you'll be able to get more intimate with your partner *and* enjoy your sensual massage sessions a lot more! If you have no inhibitions or fears and are ready to bare it all—emotionally and physically—then by all means skip this chapter. We'll catch up with you shortly.

Getting to Know You: Finding Intimacy

People often equate intimacy with sex. And while sex certainly can be an intimate experience, there are couples who engage in sex for its physical pleasure alone—even for the sport of it—without any intimacy at all. For others, intimacy is a deep place of emotional sharing and baring. That's the kind of intimacy that makes for lasting passion.

Finger Tip

How intimate a sensual massage becomes is always in your hands, whether you're the person receiving or giving the massage.

To us there are two basic forms of intimacy: physical and emotional. How close you feel or want to get with another person is your desire for intimacy. There are things that prevent intimacy, body to body or heart to heart. Maybe you can think of them as your "intimacy inhibitors." Whatever you call them, here's a chance to get to know them, then let them go. We want you to be able to enjoy all levels of intimacy!

Barriers to Physical Intimacy

Some of the most common barriers to physical intimacy for both the giver and the receiver are as follows:

♦ Hygiene

♦ Weight

♦ Moles or unusual markings

♦ Signs of abuse or previous physical harm

♦ Post-surgery scarring

♦ Hair growth or loss

♦ Signs of arousal

Barriers to Emotional Intimacy

When it comes to emotional intimacy, the following issues are often barriers:

♦ Low self-esteem, including feelings of self-doubt and inadequacy

♦ Fear, guilt, or shame about your body or how you will react to someone's touch

♦ The fear of dependency or vulnerability

♦ The fear of touch itself due to past abuse, cultural differences, or misinterpreted touch

---

Dr. Patti Says

Body image issues are one of the most common blocks to intimacy and pleasure, for both men and women, as are histories of past physical, sexual, or emotional abuse. Counseling or therapy might allow you to rediscover the joy of touch. Often the act of receiving a sensual massage by a person you trust (even love) can become a significant part of your healing process.

Overcoming Obstacles to Intimacy

The first step to overcoming obstacles to intimacy is to identify them. Once you know what's keeping you from getting close to your partner, you can work to tear down that barrier. The following exercise will help you figure out what barriers might be between you and intimacy.

Write down what triggers the following emotions (all of which are barriers to intimacy):

Fear (For example: I am scared that I may cry; I'm afraid that I'll get an erection and feel ashamed of myself.):

_____

_____

_____

Guilt (For example: I'll feel terribly guilty about being 30 pounds overweight.):

_____

_____

_____

Shame (For example: I'm ashamed of the stretch marks I have all over my breasts; no man will find me attractive.):

_____

_____

_____

Now that you've identified the obstacles, take some time to think about strategies that you can use to overcome at least one of your answers for each emotion.

Fear (For example: To overcome my fear of getting an erection, I will turn down the lights during the massage.):

_____

_____

_____

Guilt (For example: To overcome my shame at being 30 pounds overweight, I will go on a diet and start exercising regularly.):

_____

_____

_____

Shame (For example: To overcome my shame over my stretch marks, I will discuss my feelings about them with my partner and ask him to accept me as I am.):

_____

_____

_____

By taking action, you're already halfway to overcoming those obstacles!

Full Esteem Ahead!

If you don't feel very good about yourself, you're probably not going to want to put your naked body into someone else's hands. Low self-esteem is an all-too-common barrier to intimacy. The following exercise will help you to boost your self-esteem.

Ask yourself the following questions and then write down your answers.

What is one thing I could do to make me feel more connected to others right now? (Example: I could call my friend Mary and go out to lunch on the spur of the moment today …):

_____
_____
_____

What is one quality that I possess that I admire in others? (Example: I am a great friend and reliable in times of crisis ...):

_____
_____
_____

What is one thing I know I can do well? (Example: I know that under stress I can come through at my job ...):

_____
_____
_____

What is one model that I can rely on to give me strength and courage when I falter? (Example: I can watch or re-watch that movie _Gladiator_ and identify with the courage of Maximus ...):

_____
_____
_____

What are two actions I can take this week to raise my self-esteem? (Example: Get a manicure; practice my yoga ...):

_____
_____
_____

What are two thoughts that can raise my self-esteem? (Example: Remember that I am a loving sister; think about my goals and what I can do to achieve them ...):

_____
_____
_____

These questions are all directed at raising your self-esteem. They are intended to steer your thoughts from those of self-doubt to those that make you feel good about yourself. Whenever you feel your self-esteem slipping, take action: Do something that pops you up to a good level of self-esteem. You have the power to do just that.

Truth or Dare: Body Image Self-Assessment

This is a wonderful chance to find out what you really think of your body. Checking in with yourself now and then helps to challenge your thinking about yourself and helps you help yourself to overcome body image issues. If you feel up to the task, you can share what you find out about yourself with your partner. At first it may be intimidating, but disclosing your true feelings about yourself to your partner will create intimacy between you and your partner, and greater intimacy leads to a better sensual massage (and vice versa).

If you are single and your sensual massage partner doesn't exist yet, focus on how you can improve your body image just for you. For example, you may look in the mirror and see only your "thunder thighs," which you hate. Honest acknowledgement of your feelings will help pave the way to self-acceptance of just the way you are or be that pivotal moment to propel you into action to change what you see.

In the following exercise, read the questions and write down the first answers that you think of. Be sure to avoid self-censorship. Write at least two things for each of the three questions. If you are doing this with your partner, after you have both finished the quiz, you may want to share your answers with one another. Then again, you may want to keep this private, which is fine by us. It's best if you do this over coffee or a tall Bloody Mary, in neutral territory or where you feel safe and protected to do such intimate disclosure.

What I like the least about my body is (example, my breasts are too small; my butt is too fat; my eyes are squinty):

_____

_____

_____

What I like the most about my body is (example, the smooth feel of my skin; my tight tummy; my curvy lines):

_____

_____

_____

I wish I could change the following about my body (example, lose 10 pounds; gain weight on my legs; get a new hairstyle):

_____

_____

_____

This exercise may feel too scary to do with a newcomer to your love life. You may want to do it with clothes on and skate lightly on the surface. Or skip it altogether until you feel more secure with your partner to share this intimate, self-revealing information. Or just forget about it and get busy with prepping for your massage.

Take time to reflect on what you learn from this exercise. You might just find that it's amazing as a healing, revealing way to get in touch with your feelings about your body before you bare it in the raw.

> **Ouch!**
>
> If you decide to share your answers to the Truth or Dare exercise with your partner, be prepared to experience an array of emotions, including grief, shame, or fear. Your repressed emotions and memories may come flying to the surface. Handle them gently. If you cannot overcome your emotions, talk with a counselor.

The Exchange Game: Giving and Receiving Pleasure

Surprisingly, one of the greatest barriers to intimacy in a sensual massage is the inability to surrender to the act of receiving. Yes, we know, it seems strange. You're probably thinking, "What do you mean? Everyone finds it pretty easy to lie down and let the good stroking begin on their aching limbs or on that tight shoulder, right?" Well, we've found in our many years of practice that, in fact, men and women both have trouble receiving. Receiving, after all is said and done, is an exquisite act of letting go, surrendering to someone else, and trusting while you do.

Ready to practice surrendering yourself to the gift of massage with your partner? Here's a simple exercise to try (flip a coin to decide who gets to receive first):

Ask your partner to lie down with his head on a surface you choose (a bed, your lap, the couch). Tell him to close his eyes and to concentrate on just two things: Feeling the pleasant physical sensations, and receiving. Assure him that it's fine to let go of all other thoughts.

> **Dr. Patti Says**
>
> The splendor of surrendering to the present moment can't be beat. There is nothing sweeter than the act of letting go. Did you know that the French call an orgasm (okay, I had to sneak in a little tidbit about sex, here) "le petit mort"? That means the little death. That's because at orgasm you *really* surrender to the act of letting go.

You, too, can get into the exchange game and take turns with a sensual head rub, like Trista and Gene are doing—sealed with a kiss, no less!

(Robert Dunlap)

For five minutes non-stop, caress his head. Rub slowly from the forehead to the back of his neck, top to bottom, all around the hairline (or former hairline), concentrating on sending caring, tender energy to him. Make this solely for his pleasure, not yours. (You may be surprised to find that it also gives you pleasure to be the giver.) Take your time and go slowly.

After five minutes, switch roles. Be sure to thank each other for the gift of the head rub.

Once you've each given and received the head rub, take some time to discuss whether it was easier to give or to receive, and why. Use the knowledge that you gained from this exercise the next time you give each other a sensual massage.

Geography Lessons

Time for some fun. One way to learn about your partner's body and thereby get more intimate with it, inside and out, is to become its artistic recorder. Really, we mean business here: We want you to draw, paint, photograph, or sculpt one another's bodies! But for heaven's sake, don't think that you have to be a Michelangelo to do this.

Finger Tip

You don't have to haul out the art supplies to do this activity. Instead, you can describe his or her body out loud. The important thing is to look at your partner in a new way and to see things you haven't noticed before.

First, pick a medium and gather the appropriate supplies. Maybe to start out you want to do a pencil sketch of your partner; or maybe you want to go all out and create an oil portrait or a life-size sculpture. It's your call (although good luck getting your partner to model long enough for you to do a life-size sculpture!). Ultimately, the medium doesn't matter. The purpose of the activity isn't the art itself; rather, the act of re-creating your partner's body is a way to get you to take a close look at it, to really *see* him or her. You will begin to discover those little cracks, crevices, curves, dimples, straight lines, shadows, and all the various shapes and lines that make up the human body form.

Next, ask your partner to disrobe and lie down on the bed, floor, or massage table. You can decide which way you want her, faceup or -down. Have her lie in the position you request, facing the direction you set. Light the area with auxiliary lighting, such as a spotlight or table lamp, or use the natural light from a nearby window. Now study your partner's body—really scrutinize it—and then create an image of it.

When you finish your portrait, switch roles and start again.

After you both have created your portraits, share them with each other. Talk about the discoveries you made. Ask yourselves some questions: What did you notice for the very first time about the other person's body? What surprised you? What emotions did you experience? What did you feel like doing after you created the image?

Be gentle and honest with each other in your disclosures about how this process made you feel. Hopefully this exercise has made you feel closer to your partner. You have just experienced another dimension of how sensual massage, or its preparations, can enhance or reinforce your capacity for intimacy.

The Least You Need to Know

- ◆ Bodies talk without words; learn their language.
- ◆ It's often harder to receive than to give.
- ◆ You can learn to observe and discover your partner's body.
- ◆ Intimacy can be blocked by body concerns or emotional issues.
- ◆ You may be able to overcome fear, guilt, and shame through sensual massage.

Part 5

Going Wild

Massage is the ultimate aphrodisiac. The first two chapters in this section take you to the far end of the touch continuum to explore the erotic side of touch. We teach how you to build anticipation for the massage experience and how to stroke your way to sexual pleasure.

If sex isn't on your agenda, then turn to the final chapter, where we wrap things up.

Getting Into the Mood

In This Chapter

- ◆ Suggestions for the perfect date night together
- ◆ How to include water for sensual play
- ◆ The art of the striptease and how to do it
- ◆ Tips for weekend getaways

We believe that preparation for sensual massage is just as important as the touch experience itself. We've already covered the things that you can do to ready your space and prepare yourself emotionally. Now we're going to explore what you can do to set the right mood for the massage. This kind of preparation is akin to the power of foreplay for sex. The key element is anticipation.

Date Night: The Lure

First, make a date with your partner. Pick a night in the next week or so when you and your partner can clear the decks your calendars, that is. Be generous in planning for your time together. Remember, this is a prelude to a sensual massage. This time is for connecting and intimacy.

Allow yourselves plenty of time for transition from your normal activities to playtime. Maybe you are returning from a horrendous freeway commute (can you tell we're based in L.A.?), slogging it out on the sales floor, or piloting a commercial jet from 10 hours away from home. Setting aside enough time to relax, plan, and prepare for your date is a must. And if your day consists of taking care of your little brood, clear the roost for "Mommy and Daddy" to reclaim the castle for the grown-ups. We give you permission.

Finger Tip

Date night is designed as foreplay for the sensual massage itself, not necessarily as a commitment for doing one.

The Basic Questions

You may want your pre-massage date to be dinner at a romantic restaurant or a walk along the beach, or you may even be feeling frisky enough to go to an adult venue or meet in a high-end bar for drinks. You may want it to be a friendly sharing of what's new with you or an intimate time for exchanging "I love you's," or you may want to have it be a special time to honor your relationship. Maybe you want to go really wild and take this book along with you to a weekend getaway motel or spa and follow it up with touch. You decide. Make this a planned event.

Some guided questions might help you to decide when and where to get together:

- What kind of date do we want?

- Where do we prefer to have it?

- When is the best time to set aside?

- How would we like to use this date as foreplay for sensual massage?

- What outcomes would we like to experience?

Dr. Patti Says

How about meeting your partner in a public place, pretending to be strangers? I often coach couples to try this one out to rekindle their relationship fires. It works! The sheer idea of being picked up by a stranger can ignite passion. Plus, for long-term couples, I always find their preparation for even one date can go a long way in rekindling their desire to be together. You could wear different clothing or jewelry, hide in a dark corner of a bar or restaurant, or flirt with other people. Or don't tell your partner where you'll be; instead, send clues in the mail or by e-mail that indicate where to find you. (Make them good clues; the last thing you want is to spend an evening by yourself while your partner searches around town for you!) The more you invest in the playful part of your relationship (and the more you can connect with what brought you together in the first place), the better your chances for making your date a smash hit!

In the previous chapter we discussed the power of using rituals to enhance your experience. You may want to try any of these tried-and-true dating rituals:

- ◆ **Sharing a meal:** Set aside time and space to share food together.

- ◆ **Wine and Roses:** Buy a bouquet of red roses and treat yourselves to some classy red wine. Make a toast to your relationship.

- ◆ **Dress up:** Go shopping for some new "dress up" clothes to wear on your date. Pick out styles that you admire but have never worn before. If you don't want to spend a lot of money, try secondhand or consignment shops.

Concentrate on activities that allow you to be physically close to one another and select places where you can talk freely without a lot of interruptions. Instead of going to a movie after dinner on the town, why not go out dancing or take a walk on the beach or down a pretty boulevard? Or pack a gourmet picnic and take a hike in the woods.

Skinny Dipping

Nothing builds anticipation better than a shared bath before a sensual massage. Not only will it put you in the mood, it also gives you a chance to ready your bodies for the massage. Rent a hotel room with a Jacuzzi tub or use your own bathtub or shower.

Consider having the following items on hand for your bath:

- ◆ Scented oils, beads, bubbles, or salts for the water

- ◆ Loofahs, sea sponges, and bathing mitts to use on each other's bodies

- ◆ A bathtub pillow for your head

- ◆ Toys and other playful items, such as a rubber ducky, a risqué toy, a shower massage head attachment

- ◆ After-bath care products, including body powders and lotions, elegant plush robes, a satin boudoir cover-up, silk shorts, high heeled slippers with a poof of feathers at the toes, or a heat lamp for comfy drying

 Ouch!

There's nothing relaxing or romantic about a dirty bathroom or bathtub ringed with soap scum. Take some time to clean your bathroom before you bathe together.

Talk about sensual! A sensual bath can be just what you want to get close.

(Robert Dunlap)

Burlesque Time

Now that you're squeaky clean, it's time to get a little dirty—figuratively speaking. For centuries, from the hula dancers of Polynesia to the belly dancers of the Middle East and on to the "Can Can girls" of gay Paree, erotic dancing has been a reliable way to prepare one's mind and body for the delights of the flesh. Whether you plan to have an amazing evening of sex after your sensual massage or you just plain want to loosen up those joints and lubricate the options for fun and frolic, consider learning how to tease—striptease, that is—with your body in motion.

Break out of the old grind.

(Robert Dunlap)

First, it's important to forget everything you've thought about yourself up until now. That means, don't say things to yourself like "I am too old, too fat, and too reserved to let go of my body and do the wild stripping thing." Nope. We are your cheerleaders.

This is all about looking, feeling, and being *sexy*. The more you can layer items of clothing, with the slinkiest and barest at the bottom of the pile touching your skin, the better your strip show will be.

Bump Up the Volume

Some of the moves for a good striptease show include the following steps:

Choose your music before you begin. Pick a number from a CD that turns you on. Better yet, find a campy burlesque CD at your local music store.

Pick out an outfit to wear (and later take off). This can be anything from your huggy slippers and cozy flannel pj's, to a slinky array of pull-offs that dazzle, entice, and make you sizzle on the dance floor.

Here are some props for you women that you can take off layer by layer:

Finger Tip

The art of stripping has seen a revival in recent years. Many health and exercise clubs now offer lessons in stripping for women who want to learn how to groove, grind, and hump it. Stripping is great for seduction, but it's also a fun way to get yourself into shape.

- Long gloves—the silkier the better

- Sexy bottoms or undergarments, such as a teddy, fitted camisole, sheer panties, or a thong

- A jacket or bustier to cover up what's underneath

- A hoist-up bra

- A dress, gown, or other long garment that zips up the front or back, loose enough to fit over everything else

- Traditional thigh-high stockings with a garter belt—the blacker and lacier the better

- Stilettos or other really high heels

And don't forget some fun jewelry, such as flashy bracelets or tummy belts; hats, even those with rhinestones or feathers; capes, shawls—anything that adds yet another layer to take off.

Here are some ideas for the male side of stripping:

- Layered clothing, especially formal attire, such as a tux with all the trimmings, taking it off s-l-o-w-l-y.

- A tank top over those buff shoulders or chest.

- Hip-hugging cotton briefs that show everything—well almost.

- Slinky satin shorts that allure, in red, gold or black.

- A thong!

- Uniforms—especially whole body outfits such as those worn by soldiers, firefighters, and police. Don't forget the hat!

- Cowboy hat and chaps, period.

> **Goddess Helen Says**
>
> Sometimes covering up a part of the anatomy is more erotic than naked flesh. Sporting a high-neck, black-lace bodice can be just as alluring as an open front. Adding jewelry to your bared body is a real turnon for many men (and the women who wear them). Try to find a tummy belt with tiny trinkets on it that will wiggle when you walk and tinkle when you jiggle.

Any place that makes you feel alive enough to gyrate is a good place for your stripping debut. Even the dining room table, the bedroom in front of those mirrored sliding closet doors, or on the (private) backdoor patio. You get to choose the location.

Take It Off!

We recommend that you practice in front of a full-length mirror before you begin to swing those hips before your partner. Practicing your take-off act will make you feel more comfortable when curtain time finally arrives. The more you practice, the easier the strip will be. The idea is for you to do this with ease so that your partner will be panting for more … er, make that less!

Your moves might include wiggling your upper body, swinging and rotating your hips, and extending your hands to your viewer and rubbing them on your own body. Use all of your movements and body parts as part of the tease.

Practice taking your clothes off, one item at a time, slowly. Did you read that? S-l-o-w-l-y is key. The slower you remove the cover-up, the greater the teasing effect.

Make your gestures, your facial expressions, and your bodily movements as suggestive as you can. Sweetly blow kisses to your private audience as you touch your own hot spots, caress your own body, and remove each piece with deliberate, s-l-o-w and teasing motions. Even making little sounds of moaning and cooing can help.

When you are undressed to the point that makes you feel like you have stripped far enough, create a final flourish and gesture with your index finger for your partner to come get his or her sensual massage

He or she will be putty in those hands of yours. And as if that's not enough, you can strip the clothing off your lover just as deliberately, slowly, and intently as you took yours off. What a perfect ending to a good show.

> **CAUTION**
>
> **Ouch!**
>
> If you haven't been to a gym since you thought that Richard Simmons was a mattress company or you thought that Pilates was a character from the Bible, time to rethink your planned dance routine. Get fit first. Ease into action before you attempt to practice stripping.

Lost Weekend

By now you must be getting pretty steamed up. If you tried the striptease in earnest, then good for you. Maybe you're ready to take your show on the road for a weekend getaway! New settings often put people in the mood for the intimate touch of sensual massage.

Try these ten sensual getaway ideas.

♦ **Ocean cabana:** Rent a room at a hotel or resort by the ocean. Spend time in a cabana by the surf, listening to the sound of the crashing waves, smelling the salty tides, and basking in the warmth of the sun.

♦ **Spa luxury:** Book yourself into a luxury spa. Have a facial, a body wrap, a deep tissue or Shiatsu massage, hang out in the mud bath, eat vegetarian meals, and work out until you drop.

♦ **Mountain cabin:** Imagine a wintertime retreat: You and your partner sitting in a cozy cabin in front of a fire, while pure white snow covers the pines outside your window.

♦ **Poolside:** Lie by the pool at a lovely resort hotel, reading erotic novels to one another. Cool off with fresh fruity drinks or a dip in the cool waters.

♦ **Motel 8:** Even if you go low budget, make this a special time away. Laugh at the little things that are not quite luxury items, such as the plastic cups wrapped in even more plastic and the junky lamps. Let your shared laughter be your bond.

♦ **Camping:** Being in the wild can make you come alive. Use your campground for a sensual playground, bringing along the comforts of home away from home. Don't forget fluffy sleeping bags, cozy nightlights, a portable CD player, warm clothes if needed, great campfire grub, and a tent big enough to stand up in.

- **Luxury hotel or B&B:** Go all out. Rent a darling room at a luxury B&B—the more elegant the better. Allow yourselves to delve into the niceties of life, with finely prepared cuisines for snacks and breakfasts, liqueurs before reading the logbook of other guests as inspiration, and indulging in all of the creature comforts they provide for you. Treat yourself well.

- **Faraway cruise:** Set yourselves adrift on a luxury liner (some cruises now do weekend trips). Explore the isles and coves, play the on-board games, dine with total abandon, watch a crimson sunset from the upper deck, then snuggle into your bed with the gentle rolling motion to soothe you.

- **Theme resort or hotel:** Join with others in a theme experience, such as a painting course at a swank inn or a skiing weekend party. Or you may prefer a Las Vegas theme hotel. Join in the group fun, relax and enjoy your time away—really away. Even wear costumes and drink strange brews if you can.

- **At home but not at home:** Use your own home base as your kingdom or queendom for sensual getaway time. Lock the doors, unplug the computer and telephones, send the animals and children away to Grandma's for the weekend, and visit your own surroundings as though you were a guest. Let the newness and freshness of seeing this wonderful environment help turn it into a sensual paradise.

You can create a weekend getaway anywhere you choose. Get creative and commit to doing it.

The Least You Need to Know

- Even planning a pre-massage date night can bring couples closer.
- Bathing together indoors or outdoors adds sensuality to your evening.
- You don't need to be a pro to take it all off.
- Get creative with ideas for weekend getaways.

Chapter

18

For Play or Foreplay?

In This Chapter

- ◆ What's erotic to you
- ◆ The power of distance in a relationship
- ◆ Sexual response decoded
- ◆ Foreplay helpers and steamy touch tips
- ◆ Juicy ways to play it up

Foreplay is what gets you in the mood for sex. We know as well as the average Jane that foreplay takes on many forms. It can be as subtle as an e-mail lingering on your desktop asking you to meet for coffee, as sensual as a whisper in the ear, or as dramatic as a dozen long-stemmed red roses.

What turns you on—kissing, love notes, chocolates, or erotic touch—is a personal thing. Only you know that special word or action that works for you. And, by the way, what worked last Saturday night may not be what will work next weekend or next year. That's because foreplay can be as delicate as snow and as powerful as an avalanche. But no matter what form it takes, it's intended to arouse you.

We've alluded to it in earlier chapters, but in this chapter we're going to take the issue head on: If you and your partner are in agreement, you can use sensual massage as foreplay for sex. It's the ultimate arousal tool. In this chapter, we explore using the techniques and tactics of sensual massage to help you to reach sexual bliss. If that's not what you want out of your sensual massage, then we encourage you to skip to Chapter 19, where we wrap things up.

Discover Your Touch Print

Sensual massage may be the perfect gateway to erotic touch—subtle, gentle, and loving or a screaming rocketship ride into the delights of s-e-x. The next few sections may give you some great insights into sexuality and relationships and how they both really work. If you're in a committed relationship, prefer nights with an almost stranger, or long for love as a single person, you still have an erotic nature of your own. You're about to discover how to redirect your energies toward sex using sensual massage.

> **Dr. Patti Says**
>
> If you send negative messages about yourself to the world, then focus on redirecting those messages; instead, use your behavior and attitude to send out the most positive messages you can muster.

How you feel on the inside is going to dictate your sexiness on the outside. Ignore the pretty airbrushed images of women on magazine covers and learn to accept yourself, whatever dress size you pull off the rack. It's not what you look like. Instead, it's what you *feel* like. How you feel about yourself really does send a message to the outside world, telling them, "Hey, notice me. I'm a bombshell!" or "Hey, guys, I'm a blanking hunk!" Or, if you're not careful: "Don't look now, I'm not worth your glance."

Erotic is as personal as your fingerprint. What you find to be erotic may be as different as your choice of TV shows or dinner entrees. Here are some ideas for creating eroticism:

- Reading aloud a romance novel
- Watching a XXX video
- Revealing lingerie
- No lingerie
- Going out for dinner without wearing panties
- Eating dinner at home without anything on

- You are dessert
- Naked travel clubs
- Resort clubs in the Caribbean, clothing optional
- Having sex in public places
- Having sex in the car
- A glass of bubbly with your lover in front of the fireplace on a bearskin rug
- Sitting in a hot tub with your lover
- Lighting bedside candles with your lover
- Eating raw oysters in the buff
- Feeding your lover strawberries dipped in chocolate
- Blindfolding your lover and kissing afterward, all over
- Twirling your hair in front of your lover
- Licking your lips in front of your lover
- Eating a banana in front of your lover
- Eating a fig in front of your lover
- Peeling a grape for your lover
- Watching a striptease
- Doing a striptease

You're getting the idea now, aren't you? It's personal, subjective, and involves sending the message loud and clear that you might be in the mood for lovemaking. It's not about wondering whether the laundry is done yet or whether dinner is ready. It's about focus on passion, pleasure, and s-e-x.

Go over the preceding list with your lover and discuss some things and situations that may amp up your electrical charge together. Make up your own list.

Erotic Is an Inside Job

Being ready for sex goes way beyond just getting turned on by a certain look, word, or touch. Being ready for sex requires opening yourself up.

Just what is erotic? Oddly enough, it's all about that secret of foreplay, the A word again: anticipation. One of our colleagues, sexologist Dr. Jack Morin, describes eroticism in this way: For something or someone to be erotic it has to have both an attraction factor and a perceived obstacle. You are now shaking your head, aren't you, saying to yourself, "What the heck are they talking about? When I'm feeling my oats, I just unzip and go for it." But, what is it that clicks on your switch and that keeps the voltage pumping? It's what's going on in your mind, your emotional self, and yeah, down there below the belt. You have to get inside of your own erotic self and stay there for sex to work.

The formula for eroticism may work like this for you. First, he asks you out in that masculine voice of his, and you get excited about it. Or she makes a nice dinner, with wine and music, and she wears that low-cut blouse that drives you crazy for, you know … Bingo! Your eroticism switch is now in the "on" position.

Finger Tip

Sometimes not sharing all that you think and feel with a partner helps to create that feeling of eroticism. Maybe keeping some of your ideas quiet is a good idea now and then.

Okay. So what about that obstacle part of Dr. Morin's definition? Believe it or not, when sex is easy, right there for you to have, or in your face 24/7, you may lose interest. After all, everyone wants what he or she can't have. The missing ingredient for most long-term relationships is longing or desire. Without desire, eroticism dies. If Dr. Morin's right, then you need to invent an obstacle, or imagine that one is already there.

One idea for creating harmless obstacles or distance between your and your partner is to take breaks from each other. Find ways to spend time apart. You will find that breaking apart the bond of togetherness may result in more play time in your bedroom, and we're not talking about folding the laundry together while watching the 11 o'clock news.

Think about what you as a couple can do to create a harmless obstacle or some healthy distance. Focus on what you can do right now, this week, or the next. Don't let this slide too far into the future. Come on, we know you're creative enough to think of something!

If too much togetherness is your reason for lack of eroticism, trade in those old familiar duties of life, like balancing the checkbook or planning the next week's meal for the kids to take to school. You are going to find that magical doors open for more intimate time and you just may have to buy an extra fire extinguisher for next to the bed or the massage table. The less you are in her face or at his every beck and call, cleaning up the bathroom stains instead of ripping open a valentine, the more desire for sex you're going to have.

Goddess Helen Says

Here are some ideas for creating distance between you and your partner:

♦ Make a coffee date with your friends.

♦ Go to a movie with a buddy.

♦ Work out at the gym on your own schedule.

♦ Take a solo business trip.

♦ Join a group on your own.

♦ Take an art or cooking class all by yourself.

Once you begin to feel that personal space open up between you, things in the bedroom will begin to heat up.

Play It Up

If you are ready to engage in the sexual part of touch, then you'd better get savvy about how sex works. Once the key is in the sexual ignition and the engines are fired up, there is a scientific pattern that all humans follow, known as the "Sexual Response Cycle." The great sexual researchers Masters and Johnson defined the cycle as having the four phases: excitement, plateau, orgasm, and resolution. Then along came Dr. Helen Singer Kaplan, who added in the preliminary part, desire. At the Institute for Advanced Study of Human Sexuality in San Francisco, they added even further to this model, embracing the truly cyclic ebbs and flows of sex, as follows:

♦ **Phase 1: Vague stirring.** You have an uh-huh feeling somewhere down below the waist. Maybe you've just watched a rerun of *Braveheart* and Mel Gibson has your heart pounding.

♦ **Phase 2: Desire rears its head.** You feel a little warm now. Maybe you are tossing your head coquettishly. You have more than a passing interest in your object of sexual desire and are beginning to think about the possibility that this could lead to sex.

♦ **Phase 3: Excitement.** This is when the body kicks into a state of sexual arousal. Things start to happen, blood starts flowing to the genitals, your skin starts to get flushed, your breathing picks up pace, certain areas are beginning to feel a little wetness. You are thinking, "He's turning me on, oh boy ..."

Touch Term

Foreplay—The actions or behaviors that lead to sexual intercourse. Of course, they are sensual, sexual, erotic activities that are fine in their own right and may never lead to sex. They include behaviors such as deep kissing, fondling, caressing, and all kinds of genital contact. The term foreplay implies there is more to happen in that particular sexual act. The secret to foreplay is *anticipation*.

◆ **Phase 4: Plateau.** This is a state of high arousal—the peak at the top of which you freefall from the sky. Unfortunately, this is the place where many women get stuck and cannot proceed to phase 5.

◆ **Phase 5: Orgasm.** This is the big bang or the small whimper that indicates a release of the built-up blood flow, sexual tension, and energy.

◆ **Phase 6: Resolution.** The bodily changes from arousal now subside. Things go back to their formerly normal state. All quiet on the Western front.

◆ **Phase 7: What's next?** After a break, (called for men the refractory period, when the capacity to have another erection resumes) you both think, maybe talk, about going at it again … and again?

Your sensual massage can trigger any of these sexual response phases. And by the way, if you hit those end points after an orgasm, the "Resolution" or the "What's next?" phases, sensual massage can restart you for more sex.

Still not sure whether your partner is turned on? Look for any of these signs:

◆ Deep, wet, kisses on the lips

◆ Heavy breathing

◆ Hands on the genitals

◆ Touching the breasts

◆ Saying "I want you" or "I lust you"

◆ Pelvic lifting or thrusting

◆ Feelings of warmth in the chest region

◆ Skin flush especially on the chest

◆ Darkening color of areolas on the breasts

◆ Genital swelling and/or wetness

◆ An erect penis

- Arching one's back to touch

- Sweaty palms as the receiver

- Hard nipples

- Curling toes or fingers

- Fullness, heat or tingling in your genitals

- Pelvic pressure

Dr. Patti Says

A sensual foot bath makes for an incredible aphrodisiac. Place your lover's bare feet in a tub of warm soapy water. In dim lighting, with soothing music playing and incense and candles glowing, massage your partner's feet for 10 to 20 minutes. Using a slow, gentle touch, caress one foot at a time as if it were the foot of a god. After the bath anoint your partner's feet with oil. Most people feel an intense emotional connection while doing this.

Arousal Helpers

You may wonder why anyone would need an *aphrodisiac* with sensual massage. It can be quite enough to propel you into a sexual encounter, waking up your senses. Couples can get stuck without sexual desire even after hours of sensual stroking and rubbing with nice warm oils and all the trimmings. Aphrodisiacs come in handy before, during, or after a sensual massage to take it to the sexual realm. Libidos sometimes need a boost.

People have long known that objects that resemble the sexual anatomy, such as sensuous fruits (peaches) and vegetables (cucumbers), have erogenous power. And powerful animals such as the tiger, hart, and the rhinoceros are highly prized in some cultures for certain body parts, such as antlers or penises, which are believed to possess transferable sexual powers. But you don't have to walk the wilds of Africa or destroy the horns of cherished species to find an aphrodisiac for your sensual massage. No. It's quite likely that right there in your own kitchen you'll find something to get you or your partner turned on.

Touch Term _____

Aphrodisiac—a potent ingredient that aids in sexual arousal.

The following is a list of household items that have aphrodisiac qualities:

- **Chocolate.** Associated with romance, chocolate does have trace amounts of a chemical that is a natural amphetamine found in human brains, phenyl ethylamine or PEA, which makes you feel "in love."

- **Diet drinks.** Diet sodas rely on artificial sweeteners, some of which convert into PEA.

- **Oysters.** Desired for their ability to stimulate the sexual senses, the texture of these raw nibbles call to mind genitalia, and they contain zinc, which is believed to enhance reproductive capacities.

- **Honey.** The sugars in honey give fuel to the cells, including sperm.

- **Wine.** A glass or two of wine can make you more relaxed, thereby decreasing sexual inhibitions.

- **Red roses or other red flowers.** The color red connotes passionate love, with red flowers of all kinds serving as symbols of romance, passion, and love.

- **Herbal teas.** Natural teas work to stimulate, calm, or balance the body systems. Use ginseng for tonic effect, avena sativa for hormonal activation, saw palmetto for hormonal balancing, and kava kava for relaxation.

- **Aromatic oils.** Essential oils, such as ylang ylang, jasmine, sandalwood, and rose, are reputed to affect romantic feelings; cinnamon is known to stimulate the blood and awaken the senses.

- **Colors.** Certain hues evoke romance, such as rose, pink, or red.

- **Romantic music.** Melodies or musical lyrics, such as the crooning of Sinatra, classic love songs, Broadway show tunes, operatic arias, or poignant ballads affect your romantic state.

- **Charms.** Trinkets and charms, such as a photo of a loved one, a napkin or dried flowers from your first date, or even a lock of hair—can evoke the thoughts of a lover.

- **Spells.** If you believe in them, then spells might be useful for fueling the flames of passion.

Use any of these to create the mood you wish to set or eventually to find yourself in after your sensual massage.

Strokes for Sex

Remember in Chapter 6 where we talked about those pleasure points? Those were the places on your body where it felt sooo good to be touched lightly, playfully, or even with deep probing if the intention was to turn you on. Your *oohs* and *ahhs* may have said it all. If you want to use massage as foreplay for sex, concentrate on the areas from the neck to knees, faceup, because that big area is where the sexual action often occurs.

Any touch on the area "below the belt" is going to send a clear, direct message that it's time to think erotic, not just a friendly gesture. The pros stay away from that zone, knowing that an erection may spring up or wetness may sneak onto the sheets. For your sensual massage, if you want to get very sexy, this area is your focal point.

Dr. Patti Says

When I coach clients to have better sex, especially how to enhance their pleasure through self-touch toward orgasm, I teach these four components: (1) Intensity: How hard are you pushing or rubbing? (2) Rhythm: How fast or slowly are you moving your fingers or hands? (3) Placement: Where are you placing your fingers on your genitals? and (4) Direction: Are you moving them in an up-down, side-to-side, or circular motion? All four of these combine to assist a woman or man to focus on what exactly she/he is doing to create sensation and pleasure that ultimately may lead to a great orgasm. All of this also translates into giving and receiving a great sensual massage.

Erogenous Zones

Experts on sex often make claims that particular parts of the body are the special "zones" for erotic touch. However, any part of anybody can be erogenous. It's very personal. You may recall that erotic is just one level up from sensual along the touch continuum we mentioned in Chapter 2. Erotic touch usually leads to sexual feelings and responses, with signs of arousal for the receiver, like heavy or more audible breathing, swollen genitals, pelvic lifting, and hardening of the nipples. Sometimes the hips sway, the chest gets red, the back arches, and the tummy or thighs tighten up. If your partner reaches orgasm there may also be that funny thing called myotonia, in which the face is all scrunched up and toes or fingers curl like claws.

Here are some erogenous zones we commonly—and not so commonly—think of:

Earlobes

Lips

Breasts and nipples (for men and women)

Sides of the neck

Underarms

Back of the knee

Abdomen or belly

Genitals (outer and, of course, under the skin)

Buttocks

Inner thighs

Anywhere between the legs

How you touch may be as important as where you touch. Vary your sensations and practice with your massage partner to locate the places and types of touch that start a fire.

Tickling sensations can trigger a sexual response. Light, playful touch can be interpreted as a sexual cue. Tender, delicate touch along any pleasure point can be a turn on. Intensely rubbing or caressing a certain part of the body, especially the nipples or sexual organs, is going to be a direct hit.

Be sure to experiment with your sensual massage mate before you write in stone what is arousing and what isn't. People change. Your hot spots may shift over time, with the changes in your hormones or as you age. Make each sensual massage a unique exploration into the erogenous zones of your lover instead of relying on what happened last time or two decades ago.

Now, to sum it all up, get inventive about your massage tools. Let yourself go! Of course, your hands are your main provider of sexy stroking. But think about it. You also have other body parts you can use. Whether you choose to drag your hair across his hot panting chest, or even use your penis to caress over her breasts, or want to get fancy with toys or tools like the ones we talked about in Chapter 4, you can do your sensual massage in lots of different ways.

Lingual Dexterity: Tongue as Massage Tool

You can get really creative with your mouth during your sensual massage. Imagine yourself using your lingual tool to drag, lick, suck, tickle, or whatever else comes to mind on your partner's skin. Of course, if you use your tongue instead of a massage wand, your fingers or another object, you will want his skin to be clean, free of perfumed oils or lotions, and slathered in only edible products. Consider some of the following tongue techniques:

- Lick off natural, consumable massage oils, such as those produced by Kama Sutra or natural vanilla oils

- Kiss your partner's toes (known as "shrimping") and feet

- Suck on her ears—lobes and all

- Suck on his fingers

- Drag your tongue around the entire contours of her body to draw a body picture

- Spell words of love on his back

- Suckle the nipples, for her or him

- Lick, suck, or nurse on the outer or inner labia (lips of the female genitals)

- Go into full sexual oral love, with tongue in or on the genitals, for him or her

> **Dr. Patti Says**
>
> One of the best commercially available lines of sensual oils, lotions, and powders is produced by Kama Sutra. These oils are edible, safe, natural, smoothly scented, and beautifully packaged. You almost don't want to open the boxes. One of my favorites is a powder that is scooped out with a delicate pearly shell for a lid.

Roll the Dice!

One of the ways that you can turn your massage into a sexual interlude is to role play before, during, and after your massage. That's right: Get dressed up and pretend you're someone else. Follow through on existing fantasies or create new ones. Here are some ideas:

- **Goddess's Delight.** It's the fifth century in ancient India at a sacred temple (or Egypt if you prefer the Pyramid theme), and you are about to enjoy the pleasures of the flesh, mind, spirit, and senses. Play new age music, light some incense and aromatherapy oils, and hang Indian or Egyptian art on the walls. Here's the fun part: Wear Indian or Cleopatra and Caesar–style costumes and adorn your bodies with tinkling bracelets, anklets, toe rings, or belly-dancing belts made of shimmering Indian silks and gold coins. If you have a sacred altar, place theme-related items on it, such as Tibetan bells and statues of Hindu or Egyptian gods and goddesses.

Ouch!

This is one section where two key words really count: Adult and consent. If you are not legally an adult yet, then role-playing is not for you. If you and your partner want to explore the darker realms of sensual play or sexual experimentation, an explicit agreement is important before you touch a hair, light a black candle, or don a cape. This type of fantasy play may never be for you.

◆ **Erotic Faire.** Welcome to medieval times, where hearty, bawdy, earthy ways open you up to new experiences. Ladies, find some dresses that leave your cleavage heaving; guys, go for those oh-so-revealing tight trousers. Role play Robin Hood and Maid Marian, or maybe the lord and the chambermaid. Drink wine or mead out of large goblets and eat crusty breads. Have a jousting good time.

◆ **Dark Shadows.** Take a ride to the dark side. Role play as Dracula and his vampire bride (think *Interview with the Vampire* with Tom Cruise and Brad Pitt). Or experiment with some "S&M lite" using scarves to bind wrists, shoelaces to tie feet to the bed, or just hold down your lover (always with his or her consent, of course) while you administer your sensual touch.

Try dress up and erotic play to boost your temperature for more.

(Robert Dunlap)

Invent your own fantasy map of where you want to go next. Fortunately, the territory is limitless.

Sometimes the best sensual massage is the one you give to your dude over your favorite bedspread while watching reruns from hit shows of the seventies. Remember, your most cherished times of exchanging sensual massage will reflect who you both are at that time in your life. We urge you to try what you think will add sparkle and charge to your sessions. Be as creative as you can be. The more you invest in your wild ride, the better the journey.

Pre-Massage Sex?

Wild as it may seem, sometimes it's a good idea to have sex *before* your massage. (Of course, we're talking about adults in consenting relationships here.) If you are debating whether or not to have a little round of whoopee before you do your handiwork on the sensual massage table, consider these benefits:

- It will relieve the sexual tension (aching to release down there), allowing you to relax and focus on the sensuality of the massage itself.

- It will give you a sense of calm, release, and tranquility.

- It will enhance your level of sensations. Honestly, if you have an orgasm before your massage, all of your senses will be heightened.

- It will let you experience the chance for deeper, more loving intimacy before you explore the joys of sensual touch.

- It will open you up spiritually, as orgasm often sends you into a state of surrender—a lovely state for a sensual massage.

- It's the perfect sleep remedy for *after* your sensual massage.

Of course, having sex before a sensual massage isn't always appropriate. Even though your raging hormones are screaming in your lower belly, "Let's *gooo* ..." your mind and heart may not be ready to align with your basest desires. Besides, we've already explained that the secret for great sex is anticipation—it's one of the best forms of foreplay there is. The state of longing, wishing for, and thinking about what may happen can electrify the experience. Why push it? You can always decide to let your anticipation be your muse while you sensually touch on top of the sheets before you scoot in between them for the night.

The Least You Need to Know

- ◆ Your eroticism is unique and subjective.

- ◆ Sensual massage can put you into the sexual response cycle.

- ◆ You can use massage as foreplay for sex.

- ◆ Access your wild side using sensual massage.

Chapter 19

Wrapping It Up

In This Chapter

- ◆ How to say thanks
- ◆ Finding the sacred path of love
- ◆ Your feedback guide
- ◆ Keeping love alive

Each time you give and receive a sensual massage you will want to tune in to your partner and talk about what you both just experienced. That's the only way you'll both know what worked, what didn't work, and how to make it even better the next time. Be sure to set aside time after your massage to talk about how it felt.

How Was It for You?

Consider asking your partner the following questions after your massage:

- ◆ How well do you feel that we met our intentions?

    Example: I feel so relaxed …

Finger Tip _____

Don't judge yourself during a sensual massage. It is a time to give and receive touch. Period.

♦ What body parts felt the best to be touched?

Example: I loved the scalp massage ...

♦ What massage strokes or areas made you feel uncomfortable?

Example: I get a little ticklish when you rub between my toes ...

♦ What was your favorite part to have touched?

Example: I loved how you massaged my upper legs ...

♦ What would you like more of next time?

Example: Next time you could spend more time on my arms and hands ...

♦ What would you like less of next time?

Example: Maybe a little less on my face ...

♦ How are you feeling right now?

Example: I can't wait to kiss you ...

♦ What's next for us?

Example: What are your plans for the next hour, darling?

♦ Ready for your next sensual massage yet?

Example: What are you doing tomorrow night?

Giving and getting feedback about your sensual massage session will enhance your self-confidence, your connection with your partner, and your ability to bathe in those feel-good sensations that can catapult your body into ecstasy.

More Than Words of Thanks

Each time that you conduct a sensual massage you have an opportunity to center into that experience. You just learned how to get and give feedback to improve your methods and find out how things worked or didn't. Now, you get to focus on your partner and your inner self and to explore the emotional or spiritual benefits.

Using the focusing techniques we described in Chapter 15, concentrate on your inner thoughts and feelings as they relate to your partner. Now, ask yourself this question:

What did I appreciate about this experience? Was it to be totally alone with your partner, whom you know and love, in this quiet, sensual, maybe even sexy way? Was it the fact that you two had no other distractions other than sharing physical pleasure for two hours? Let the answers rise within you like doves gliding on air currents.

Now concentrate on your partner and ask yourself this question: *What was one thing about my partner and this process that made me feel appreciative?* It could be the way that she looked you in the eyes while you touched her face. Or maybe he cooed when you gave him the head massage. Maybe the sheer tenderness of the experience made you feel more intimate and connected to your partner. It could be that for months or years now you two haven't spent uninterrupted quiet time together and this experience rekindled something wonderful. Or maybe you both got to explore a ritual that strengthened your spiritual bond. Then again, maybe you found that raunchy part of your relationship that has fired up the sizzle that you've been missing. All of these can happen during a sensual massage.

The key here is to tap into what you feel now and what you felt during the sensual massage, and to share those feelings with your partner. Even if all you felt was gratitude for time away from the kids or the pleasure of flesh on flesh, tell that to your partner.

Goddess Helen Says

Here's a closing ritual that you can try:

Place some photos of you and your partner together on your altar (or next to the massage table if you don't have an altar), along with some candles and floral buds (not fully blossomed ones) to show the potential for blooming. If you are married, place your wedding rings there, too. When you finish your massage, hold up the floral buds, link your arms, look into one another's eyes, and say, "I honor the beauty of your soul and give thanks to have you in my life." That should give you lasting love and seal the bonding of your massage.

Early on in this book we said that touch is essential for life. Most humans are touch-deprived and touch-starved. Make sure that you make the time and space for touch, to ensure a long and healthy life. And let's not forget that keeping up a habit of sensual massage will put a radiant smile on your face as you creak into bed at 90 with oils by your bedside, music playing, and your honey at your side. Pleasure is your divine birthright. Celebrate it while you can.

The Road from Eros to Love

Many couples will want to use this book for sharing touch just for the sake of the pleasure it gives. Others may want to explore this journey to their best orgasm yet. You may fit into either or both of those categories. There is yet one more option, and that is to move yourself along the road to greater love.

Many great teachers on love and spirituality talk about the honoring that takes place in a sacred and loving relationship. Calling your partner a beloved is one step in that process. Doing rituals for increasing your bond of love is another step. And sharing sacred and intimate touch with a beloved may elevate your relationship to new ground. It's your attitude, your indulgence in the emotional and spiritual enrichment of your relationship, and, of course the giving and receiving of touch that lets love flourish.

If you are in a long-term relationship, this week see your partner as your true beloved. Honor her or him with your intentions, your words, your praise, and your emotional extension of caring and adoration. Why not send a card showing your love or do something you've never done before? Take over all of the household duties for one day or bring her breakfast in bed, hold his hand at the movies or buy a new car as a surprise.

The Four Secrets of Lasting Love

Sensual massage may be just what you have been wishing for in your lives as a couple. Why? Because the very act of giving unconditionally to a partner can send shivers of delight not only up the spine but into the heart of your beloved. Touch can be used to build a solid foundation of love. And love must be tended, nurtured, and nourished. That nourishment may, in fact, be your time spent in sensual touch.

In closing, here are four secrets to lasting love:

Learn all you can and educate yourself daily.

Open your heart and spirit to your full capacity.

Vary what you do by experimenting with sensual touch and avoiding sensual or sexual boredom.

Express yourself fully and discover the unique contribution that only you can make.

May you receive all the loving touch you can stand.

The Least You Need to Know

◆ Checking in after each sensual massage is important.

◆ Showing appreciation strengthens your connection with a partner.

◆ The four secrets of love ensure your success with touch.

Touch Terms

ambiance   A pleasing atmosphere for your sensual massage.

anaerobic   Without the presence of oxygen.

anticipation   The secret ingredient to foreplay, in which longing for someone or something builds excitement.

aphrodisiac   Potent ingredients that aid in sexual arousal.

approach   How you create the mood for your sensual massage, including how you talk to your partner and the way that you lay your hands on your partner's body.

aromatherapy   A form of treatment that uses the essential oils from plants and is commonly used in massage; depending on how you use it, it can have a relaxing, balancing, stimulating, or healing effect.

body alignment   Proper body positioning during your sensual massage so that the energy comes from your center of gravity.

body etiquette   Making sure the body is properly groomed before engaging in massage.

brush it   A light massage stroke using the fingertips as if you are stroking the skin with a brush or using a feather.

carrier oil   A base oil for massage, such as sesame, grape seed, or wheat germ oil.

chakra The seven energy centers in the body.

chi Life force energy.

continuum of touch The range of touch from healing to affection to sensual to erotic and sexual.

cortisol A stress hormone that massage helps to ward off.

dry skin brushing Using a natural bristle brush on dry skin to rid the skin of dead cells and increase circulation.

endorphins The "feel good" hormones that are released with massage.

erogenous Zones or places on the body that can be sexually arousing.

erotic Arousing; on the sensual touch continuum occurring between sensual and sexual touch.

essential oils Fragrant oils that are extracted from plants and herbs; can be added to carrier oil.

eye-to-eye contact An essential ingredient for feeling connected with your partner.

eye coverings Anything—from a warm washcloth to a silken eye pillow filled with aromatic herbs—used to block light and soothe tired eyes.

fantasy Movies you make in your mind.

feng shui The art of clearing and healing your space, such as your home.

foreplay Actions and behaviors that lead to sexual intercourse.

friction A massage stroke that uses circular rubbing motions like finger painting.

hara Gravity center of the body near the belly button, also called the "Tan-Den."

holistic Treating the whole organism, not just a symptom.

inhibition Shyness or other mental/emotional obstacle that could hinder your sensual massage experience.

intimacy Emotional or physical closeness; a feeling of oneness with a partner.

intention A decision for a desired outcome, something that massage partners need to decide upon before starting a sensual massage.

Kama Sutra A well-known text for lovemaking; a spiritual path to ecstasy.

knead it A massage stroke that uses squeezing and lifting motions like kneading bread.

limbic region   An area in the brain that controls the emotions.

lymph   Fluid that helps fight infection found in the lymphatic system.

mehendi   The ancient Indian practice of applying designs and patterns onto the skin using lasting though nonpermanent dyes.

Meisners corpuscles   The nerve fibers in the lips that are responsible for making lip-to-lip contact so sensuous.

mellanocytes   The cells that give the skin its coloring.

meridians   Pathways in the body that convey energy and vital force.

mood music   Slow, calming music without words, preferably instrumental, to minimize distraction.

OM   Universal sound of Life.

orgasm   Sexual climax; the peak of the sexual response cycle, also known as "the big O."

oxytocin   The hormone that both men and women secrete at orgasm, which propels feelings of bonding, intimacy, and nurturing.

pheromones   Chemicals that are released by all animals that are in part responsible for mate attraction and selection.

pranayama   A yoga technique for breathing.

reflexology   A therapy in which the feet or hands are pressed to bring relief to corresponding areas in the body.

ritual   A ceremony or celebration.

roll it   A long gliding massage stroke similar to rolling out pastry with a rolling pin.

sacred altar   An area in your home, a dresser top or end table, where you place trinkets that show the love between you and your partner, including photos, candles, or a spiritual statue.

sensual   Pleasing or opening to the senses.

tai chi   A spiritual practice using body movements.

tantra   A tradition of sacred sexual practices.

tap it   A massage stroke involving a light tapping on the skin, like tapping a drum.

trigger points   Areas in the muscle that are tender but when pressed can bring about relief.

Resources and References

You'll be able to find massage oils, tables, and tools at many of the online resources listed here. Plus, we've included contact information for many professional associations in case you want to call or write to find out more about any of the topics discussed in this book. You should also feel free to be in touch with either of us if you'd like more information.

You may contact Dr. Patti Britton by writing to 8391 Beverly Blvd, #438, Los Angeles, CA 90048; e-mail: askthesexcoach@aol.com.

You also can find out more about Dr. Patti, including her other books, videos, workshops, cruise ship seminars, media appearances, and free newsletter at the following websites:

www.yoursexcoach.com

www.ivillage.com/relationships
(Where she hosts live chats weekly and online courses.)

www.evesgarden.com
(Where she hosts a sexually informative weekly radio show.)

You can find Goddess Helen at her website: www.servethegoddess.com and luxuriate in her wisdom and book an appointment for her fabulous touch! Contact her via e-mail at Helen@servethegoddess.com or call 323-993-6055.

Professional Massage Associations

Associated Bodywork and Massage Professionals
www.abmp.com

International Massage Association
www.imagroup.com

International SPA Association
www.experiencespa.com

Feng Shui Experts

Claire Jacobs, Los Angeles
www.fleurdechi.com

Master Nate Batoon
P.O. Box 999
Anaheim, CA 92815
714-774-7550
Chiwiz999@aol.com

Massage, Sex, and Pleasure Toys, Videos, and Erotica

Sinclair Institute (videos)
www.bettersex.com

Eve's Garden (toys, books, and videos, plus Dr. Patti's weekly web radio show)
Eve's Garden
www.evesgarden.com
Retail store:
119 W. 57 St (Suite 1201)
New York, NY
1-800-848-3837

Sexuality Resource Guide (videos)
www.loveandintimacy.com

Alexander Institute (videos)
www.lovingsex.com

Temptu (body arts and temporary tattoos)
www.temptu.com

Zen Clocks (zen alarm clocks and chimes)
www.zen-clocks.com

Dr. Patti's website (toys, books, and videos)
www.yoursexcoach.com

Liberator Shapes (sex or massage cushions that you see in a lot of our photos in this book)
www.liberatorshapes.com

Libido Magazine (art and erotica)
www.libidomag.com

Other sites devoted to sex and pleasure toys, massage slippery stuff, and other neat things:

www.xandria.com

www.mypleasure.com

www.blowfish.com

www.grandopening.com

www.babeland.com

www.drugstore.com

Other sites devoted to massage oils and products:

www.massagewarehouse.com (tables, chairs, and so on)

www.dreamingearth.com

www.RedEnvelope.com

www.Massageproducts.com

www.botanical.com

www.buyaromatherapy.com

www.gaiam.com

For massage supplies, you can also call Best of Nature Massage Supply Superstore, 1-800-228-6457. Any health food store may have quality massage oils, so check around your neighborhood.

Organizations Devoted to Sexual Health and Well-Being

Institute for Advanced Study of Human Sexuality
www.iashs.edu

Planned Parenthood Federation of America, Inc.
www.ppfa.org

SIECUS (The Sexuality Information and Education Council of the U.S.)
www.siecus.org

Society for Scientific Study of Sexuality
www.ssss.org

Tantric sexuality
www.tantra.org

Sex Therapists/Counselors

American Board of Sexology and the American Association of Clinical Sexologists
www.sexologist.org

American Association of Sexuality Educators, Counselors, and Therapists
www.aasect.org

Suggested Reading

Anand, Margo. *The Art of Sexual Ecstasy: The Path of Sacred Sexuality for Western Lovers.* New York, NY: Putnam Books, 1989.

Britton, Patti, Ph.D. *The Adventures of Her in France.* Beverly Hills, CA: Leopard Rising, 2001.

Brockway, Laurie Sue, Rev. *A Goddess Is a Girl's Best Friend: A Divine Guide to Finding Love, Success, and Happiness.* New York, NY: Perigee Books, 2003.

Budilovsky, Joan, and Eve Adamson. *The Complete Idiot's Guide to Massage.* Indianapolis, IN: Alpha Books, 1998.

Cabot, Laurie, with Tom Cowan. *Love Magic: The Way to Love Through Rituals, Spells, and the Magical Life.* New York, NY: Barnes & Noble Books, 1992.

Crenshaw, Theresa L., M.D. *The Alchemy of Love and Lust: How Our Sex Hormones Influence Our Relationships*. New York, NY: Pocket Books/Simon & Schuster, 1996.

Dolnick, Barrie, Julia Condon, and Donna Limoges. *Sexual Bewitchery: And Other Ancient Feminine Wiles*. New York, NY: Avon Books, 1998.

Endacott, Michael. *The Encyclopedia Of Alternative Health & Natural Remedies*. Italy: Carlton Books Limited, 1996.

Fulghum, Robert. *All I Really Need to Know I Learned in Kindergarten: Uncommon Thoughts on Common Things*. New York, NY: Fawcett Publications/Random House, 1988.

George, Leslie. *Bath and Beauty and the Fine Art of Pampering Oneself*. New York, NY: Hearst Communications, Inc., 1998.

Gray, John, Ph.D. *Men are from Mars, Women are from Venus*. New York, NY: HarperCollins, 1992.

Kapit, Wynn and Lawrence M. Elson. *The Anatomy Coloring Book*, second edition. New York, NY: HarperCollins, 1993.

Kennedy, Adele P. and Susan Dean, Ph.D. *Touching for Pleasure: A Guide to Massage and Sexual Intimacy*. Chatsworth, CA: Chatsworth Press, 1994. (This book is only available directly from Chatsworh Press, PO BOX 4326, Chatsworh, CA 91311.)

Kuriansky, Judy, Ph.D. *The Complete Idiot's Guide to Tantric Sex*. Indianapolis, IN: Alpha Books, 2001.

LaCroix, Nitya. *Tantric Sex: The Tantric Art of Sensual Loving*. New York, NY: Southwater/Anness Publishing Limited, 2001.

Leeds, Regina. *The Zen of Organizing: Creating Order and Peace in Your Home, Career and Life*. Indianapolis, IN: Alpha Books, 2002.

Lidell, Lucinda. *The Book of Massage: The Complete Step-By-Step Guide to Eastern and Western Techniques*. New York, NY: Fireside/Simon & Schuster, 2001.

Mannering, Douglas. *The Art of the Kama Sutra* (A Compilation of Works from the Bridgeman Art Library). New York, NY: Shooting Star Press, 1994.

Morin, Jack, Ph.D. *The Erotic Mind: Unlocking the Inner Sources of Sexual Passion and Fulfillment*. New York, NY: HarperCollins, 1995.

Mumford, John, Ph.D. *Ecstasy Through Tantra*. St. Paul, MN: Llewellyn Publications, 1998.

Pasahow, Carole, Ph.D. *Sexy Encounters: 21 Days of Provocative Passion Fixes*. Avon, MA: Adams Media, 2003.

Russell, Stephen and Jurgen Kolb. *The Tao of Sexual Massage*. New York, NY: Simon & Schuster, 1992.

Steinberg, David, Editor. *The Erotic Impulse: Honoring the Sensual Self*. New York, NY: Jeremy P. Tarcher/Perigee, 1992.

Strauss, Nathan B. *Shiatsu For Lovers*. Hod Hasharon, Israel: Astrolog Publishing House, 2000.

Stubbs, Kenneth Ray, Ph.D., with Louise-Andree Saulnier. *Erotic Massage: The Touch of Love*. Larkspur, CA: Secret Garden, 1999. (Secret Garden: P.O. Box 67-ECA, Larkspur, CA 94939-0067)

Tannen, Deborah, Ph.D. *You Just Don't Understand: Women and Men in Conversation*. New York, NY: Ballantine Books, 1990.

Tisserand, Maggie. *Aromatherapy for Women: A Practical Guide to Essential Oils for Health and Beauty*. Rochester, VT: Healing Arts Press, 1996.

Tisserand, Robert. *Aromatherapy To Heal and Tend The Body*. Santa Fe, NM: Lotus Press, 1998.

Tolle, Eckhart. *The Power of Now: A Guide to Spiritual Enlightenment*. Novato, CA: New World Library, 1999.

Wikoff, Johanina, Ph.D. et al. *The Complete Idiot's Guide to the Kama Sutra*. Indianapolis, IN: Alpha Books, 2000.

Worwood, Valerie Ann. *Scents & Scentuality: Aromatherapy & Essential Oils for Romance, Love and Sex*. Novato, CA: New World Library, 1999.

For recommended videos, check out Dr. Patti's website: www.yoursexcoach.com and be sure to register early for your copy of Dr. Patti's and Goddess Helen's new video on sensual massage.

Appendix C

The Gift of Massage

Give these massage coupons to your partner, then encourage the recipient to turn them in whenever he or she needs a quick pick-me-up or an entire evening of touch. For couples who lead busy lives, having reminders such as these helps them allocate time for touch and intimacy.

If you feel inspired, create your own personalized invitations. For example, you may want to invite your partner for a 20-minute sensual shower or a one-hour seduction. If sex is on your mind, be bold and invite your lover to play sexual games. Make it up. You'll be glad you did.

MASSAGE COUPONS

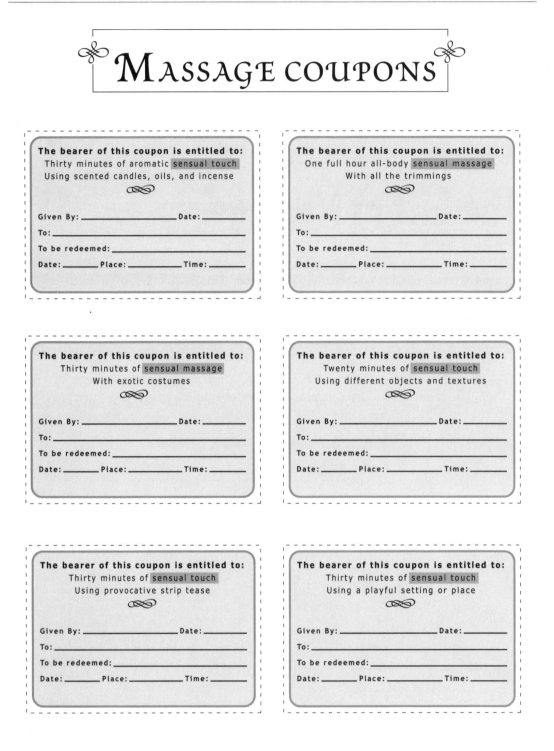

The bearer of this coupon is entitled to:
Thirty minutes of aromatic sensual touch
Using scented candles, oils, and incense

Given By: _____ Date: _____
To: _____
To be redeemed: _____
Date: _____ Place: _____ Time: _____

The bearer of this coupon is entitled to:
One full hour all-body sensual massage
With all the trimmings

Given By: _____ Date: _____
To: _____
To be redeemed: _____
Date: _____ Place: _____ Time: _____

The bearer of this coupon is entitled to:
Thirty minutes of sensual massage
With exotic costumes

Given By: _____ Date: _____
To: _____
To be redeemed: _____
Date: _____ Place: _____ Time: _____

The bearer of this coupon is entitled to:
Twenty minutes of sensual touch
Using different objects and textures

Given By: _____ Date: _____
To: _____
To be redeemed: _____
Date: _____ Place: _____ Time: _____

The bearer of this coupon is entitled to:
Thirty minutes of sensual touch
Using provocative strip tease

Given By: _____ Date: _____
To: _____
To be redeemed: _____
Date: _____ Place: _____ Time: _____

The bearer of this coupon is entitled to:
Thirty minutes of sensual touch
Using a playful setting or place

Given By: _____ Date: _____
To: _____
To be redeemed: _____
Date: _____ Place: _____ Time: _____

MASSAGE COUPONS

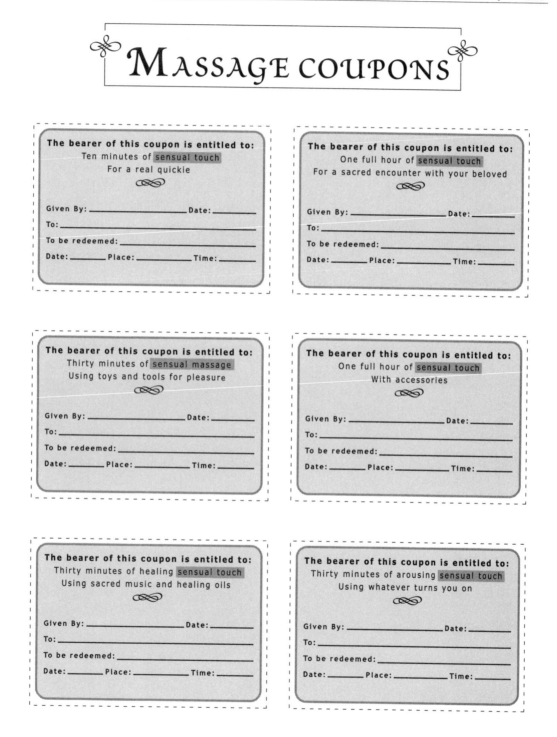

The bearer of this coupon is entitled to:
Ten minutes of sensual touch
For a real quickie

Given By: _____ Date: _____
To: _____
To be redeemed: _____
Date: _____ Place: _____ Time: _____

The bearer of this coupon is entitled to:
One full hour of sensual touch
For a sacred encounter with your beloved

Given By: _____ Date: _____
To: _____
To be redeemed: _____
Date: _____ Place: _____ Time: _____

The bearer of this coupon is entitled to:
Thirty minutes of sensual massage
Using toys and tools for pleasure

Given By: _____ Date: _____
To: _____
To be redeemed: _____
Date: _____ Place: _____ Time: _____

The bearer of this coupon is entitled to:
One full hour of sensual touch
With accessories

Given By: _____ Date: _____
To: _____
To be redeemed: _____
Date: _____ Place: _____ Time: _____

The bearer of this coupon is entitled to:
Thirty minutes of healing sensual touch
Using sacred music and healing oils

Given By: _____ Date: _____
To: _____
To be redeemed: _____
Date: _____ Place: _____ Time: _____

The bearer of this coupon is entitled to:
Thirty minutes of arousing sensual touch
Using whatever turns you on

Given By: _____ Date: _____
To: _____
To be redeemed: _____
Date: _____ Place: _____ Time: _____

Index

Dr. Patti Britton and Helen Hodgson